BLACK LEGACY PRESS™
WWW.BLACKLEGACYPRESS.ORG

Antique Works of Art from Benin
By
Augustus Henry Lane-Fox Pitt-Rivers

Copyright © 2024 by BLACKLEGACYPRESS.ORG
All rights reserved. No part of this publication may be reproduced or transmitted in any form or by any means electronic or mechanical, including information storage and retrieval systems without permission in writing from the publisher, except for student research using the appropriate citations.

ISBN: 978-1-63652-421-4

ANTIQUE WORKS OF ART FROM BENIN

Augustus Henry Lane-Fox Pitt-Rivers

CONTENTS

WORKS OF ART FROM BENIN, WEST AFRICA..............1
DESCRIPTION OF PLATE I..4
DESCRIPTION OF PLATE II. 8
DESCRIPTION OF PLATE III..11
DESCRIPTION OF PLATE IV. 14
DESCRIPTION OF PLATE V..18
DESCRIPTION OF PLATE VI...20
DESCRIPTION OF PLATE VII. 23
DESCRIPTION OF PLATE VIII. 27
DESCRIPTION OF PLATE IX. 30
DESCRIPTION OF PLATE X. 33
DESCRIPTION OF PLATE XI. 36
DESCRIPTION OF PLATE XII. 38
DESCRIPTION OF PLATE XIII. 40
DESCRIPTION OF PLATE XIV..42
DESCRIPTION OF PLATE XV. 44
DESCRIPTION OF PLATE XVI. 47
DESCRIPTION OF PLATE XVII...49
DESCRIPTION OF PLATE XVIII. 51
DESCRIPTION OF PLATE XIX. 55
DESCRIPTION OF PLATE XX...58

DESCRIPTION OF PLATE XXI. 62

DESCRIPTION OF PLATE XXII. 66

DESCRIPTION OF PLATE XXIII. 70

DESCRIPTION OF PLATE XXIV. 75

DESCRIPTION OF PLATE XXV. 80

DESCRIPTION OF PLATE XXVI. 85

DESCRIPTION OF PLATE XXVII. 91

DESCRIPTION OF PLATE XXVIII. 96

DESCRIPTION OF PLATE XXIX. 103

DESCRIPTION OF PLATE XXX. 108

DESCRIPTION OF PLATE XXXI. 114

DESCRIPTION OF PLATE XXXII. 118

DESCRIPTION OF PLATE XXXIII. 126

DESCRIPTION OF PLATE XXXIV. 131

DESCRIPTION OF PLATE XXXV. 134

DESCRIPTION OF PLATE XXXVI. 137

DESCRIPTION OF PLATE XXXVII. 142

DESCRIPTION OF PLATE XXXVIII. 145

DESCRIPTION OF PLATE XXXIX. 149

DESCRIPTION OF PLATE XL. 152

DESCRIPTION OF PLATE XLI. 157

DESCRIPTION OF PLATE XLII. 160

DESCRIPTION OF PLATE XLIII. 164

DESCRIPTION OF PLATE XLIV. 169

DESCRIPTION OF PLATE XLV. 176
DESCRIPTION OF PLATE XLVI. 182
DESCRIPTION OF PLATE XLVII. 188
DESCRIPTION OF PLATE XLVIII 190
DESCRIPTION OF PLATE XLIX. 193
DESCRIPTION OF PLATE L 198

WORKS OF ART FROM BENIN, WEST AFRICA.

OBTAINED BY THE PUNITIVE EXPEDITION IN 1897, AND NOW IN GENERAL PITT RIVERS'S MUSEUM AT FARNHAM, DORSET.

Benin is situated on the Guinea Coast, near the mouth of the Niger, in latitude 6·12 north, and longitude 5 to 6 east.

It was discovered by the Portuguese at the end of the fourteenth or commencement of the fifteenth centuries. The Portuguese were followed by the Dutch and Swedes, and in 1553 the first English expedition arrived on the coast, and established a trade with the king, who received them willingly.

Benin at that time appears by a Dutch narrative to have been quite a large city, surrounded by a high wall, and having a broad street through the centre. The people were comparatively civilized. The king possessed a number of horses which have long since disappeared and become unknown. Faulkner, in 1825, saw three solitary horses belonging to the king, which he says no one was bold enough to ride.

In 1702 a Dutchman, named Nyendaeel, describes the city, and speaks of the human sacrifices there. He says that the people were great makers of ornamental brass work in his day, which they seem to have learnt from the Portuguese. It was visited by Sir Richard Burton, who went there to try to put a stop to human sacrifices, at the time he was consul at Fernando Po. In 1892 it was visited by Captain H. L. Galloway, who speaks of the city as possessing only the ruins of its former greatness; the abolition of the slave trade had put a stop to the prosperity of the place, and the king had prohibited any intercourse with Europeans. The town had been reduced to a collection of huts, and its trade had dwindled down to almost nil. The houses have a sort of impluvium in the centre of the rooms, which has led some to suppose that their style of architecture may have been derived from the Roman colonies of North Africa.

In 1896 an expedition, consisting of some 250 men, with presents and merchandise, left the British settlements on the coast, and endeavoured to advance towards Benin city. The expedition was conducted with courage and perseverance, but with the utmost rashness. Almost unarmed, neglecting all ordinary precautions, contrary to the advice of the neighbouring chiefs, and with the express prohibition of the King of Benin to advance, they marched straight into an ambuscade which had been prepared for them in the forest on each side of the road, and as their revolvers were locked up in their boxes at the time, they were massacred to a man with the exception of two, Captain Boisragon and Mr. Locke, who, after suffering the utmost hardships, escaped to the British settlements on the coast to tell the tale.

Within five weeks after the occurrence, a punitive expedition entered Benin, on 18th January, 1897, and took the town. The king fled, but was afterwards brought back and made to humiliate himself before his conquerers, and his territory annexed to the British crown.

The city was found in a terrible state of bloodshed and disorder, saturated with the blood of human sacrifices offered up to their Juju, or religious rites and customs, for which the place had long been recognised as the "city of blood."

What may be hereafter the advantages to trade resulting from this expedition it is difficult to say, but the point of chief interest in connection with the subject of this paper was the discovery, mostly in the king's compound and the Juju houses, of numerous works of art in brass, bronze, and ivory, which, as before stated, were mentioned by the Dutchman, Van Nyendaeel, as having been constructed by the people of Benin in 1700.

These antiquities were brought away by the members of the punitive expedition and sold in London and elsewhere. Little or no account of them could be given by the natives, and as the expedition was as usual unaccompanied by any scientific explorer charged with the duty of making inquiries upon matters of historic and antiquarian interest, no reliable information about them could be obtained. They were found buried and covered with blood, some of them having been used amongst the apparatus of their Juju sacrifices.

A good collection of these antiquities, through the agency of Mr. Charles Read, F.S.A., has found its way into the British Museum; others no doubt have fallen into the hands of persons whose chief interest in them has been as relics of a sensational and bloody episode, but their real value consists in their representing a phase of art—and rather an advanced stage—of which there is no actual record, although no doubt we cannot be far wrong in attributing it to European influence, probably that of the Portuguese some time in the sixteenth century.

A. P. R.

RUSHMORE, SALISBURY,
April, 1900.

DESCRIPTION OF PLATE I.

Fig. 1.—Bronze plaque, representing two warriors with broad leaf-shaped swords in their right hands. Coral or agate head-dress. Coral chokers, badge of rank. Leopards' teeth necklace. Coral scarf across shoulder. Leopards' heads hanging on left sides. Skirts each ornamented with a human head. Armlets, anklets, etc. Ground ornamented with the usual foil ornament incised.

Fig. 2.—Bronze plaque, representing two figures holding plaques or books in front. Coral chokers, badge of rank. Reticulated head-dresses of coral or agate, similar to that represented in Plate XXI, Fig. 121. Barbed objects of unknown use behind left shoulders, ornamented with straight line diaper pattern. Ground ornamented with foil ornaments incised. Guilloche on sides of plaque.

Fig. 3.—Bronze plaque, representing three warriors, two with feathers in head-dress and trefoil leaves at top; one with pot helmet, button on top. The latter has a coral choker, badge of rank, and all have leopards' teeth necklaces. The central figure has a cylindrical case on shoulder. Two have hands on their sword-hilts. All three have leopards' heads on breast, and quadrangular bells hanging from neck. Leopards' skins and other objects hang on left sides. Ground ornamented with foil ornaments incised.

Fig. 4.—Bronze plaque, figure of warrior with spear in right hand, shield on left shoulder. Head-dress of coral or agate, similar to that represented in Plate XXI, Fig. 121. Quadrangular bell hanging from neck. Chain-like anklets. Coral choker, badge of rank, and leopards' teeth necklace. A nude attendant on right upholds a large broad leaf-shaped sword, with a ring attached to pommel. Another holds two sistri or bells fastened together by a chain. Small figure on left is blowing an elephant's tusk trumpet. Figures above in profile are holding up tablets or books. The

dress of one of them is fastened with tags or loops of unusual form. These figures have Roman noses, and are evidently not negro. Ground ornamented with the usual foil ornament incised.

DESCRIPTION OF PLATE II.

Figs. 5 and 6.—Bronze plaque, representing a warrior in centre, turned to his left. He has a beard and a necklace of leopards' teeth, but no coral choker. He has a high helmet, somewhat in the form of a grenadier cap. Quadrangular bell on neck. Dagger in sheath on right side, and various appurtenances hanging from his dress. He holds a narrow leaf-shaped sword in his right hand over an enemy who has fallen, and who has already a leaf-shaped sword thrust through his body. The victim has a sword-sheath on left side, with broad end, and a peculiar head-dress. His horse is represented below with an attendant holding it by a chain and carrying barbed darts in his left hand. On the right of the conqueror is a small figure blowing a tusk trumpet, and on his right a larger figure carrying a shield in his left hand and a cluster of weapons. He has a high helmet, ornamented with representations of cowrie shells of nearly the same form as that of the central figure. Above are two figures, one blowing what appears to be a musical instrument and the other carrying a barbed pointed implement, and armed with a sword in sheath similar to that of the fallen warrior. The plaque appears to represent a victory of some kind, and all the conquerors have the same high helmet. The ground is ornamented with the usual foil ornament incised.

Figs. 7 and 8.—Bronze plaque, representing a king or noble on horseback sitting sideways, his hands upheld by attendants, one of whom has a long thin sword in his hand in sheath. Two attendants, with helmets or hair represented by ribs, are holding up shields to shelter the king from the sun. The king or noble has a coral choker, badge of rank, with a coral necklace hanging on breast. Horse's head-collar hung with crotals. A small attendant carries a "manilla" in his hand. The two figures above are armed with bows and arrows. Ground ornamented with foil ornaments incised.

De Bry, "India Orientalis," says that in the sixteenth century both the king and chiefs were wont to ride side-saddle upon led horses. They were supported by retainers, who held over their heads either shields or umbrellas, and accompanied by a band of musicians playing on ivory horns, gong-gongs, drums, harps, and a kind of rattle.

DESCRIPTION OF PLATE III.

Fig. 9.—Bronze plaque, naked figure of boy; hair in conventional bands; three tribal marks over each eye and band on forehead. Coral choker, badge of rank. Armlets and anklets. Four rosettes on ground and usual foil ornaments. De Bry says that all young people went naked until marriage.

Fig. 10.—Bronze plaque, figure of warrior with helmet or hair represented by ribs. Leaf-shaped sword upheld in right hand. A bundle of objects on head upheld by left hand. Object resembling a despatch case on left side, fastened by a belt over right shoulder. Human mask on left side. Four fishes on ground, and the usual foil ornaments incised.

Figs. 11 and 12.—Bronze plaque, representing a figure holding a ball, perhaps a cannon ball, in front. Coral choker, badge of rank. Three tribal marks over each eye. Crest on head-dress, feather in cap. Skirt wound up behind left shoulder. Skirt ornamented with a head and hands. Four rosettes on ground, and usual foil ornaments incised. Guilloche on sides of plaque.

DESCRIPTION OF PLATE IV.

Fig. 13.—Bronze plaque, figure of warrior, feather in cap; broad leaf-shaped sword in right hand. Coral choker, badge of rank. Leopards' teeth necklace. Coral sash; ground ornamented with leaf-shaped foil, ornaments incised.

Figs. 14 and 15.—Bronze ægis or plaque, with representations of two figures with staves in their right hands. Coral chokers, badge of rank. On the breasts are two Maltese crosses hanging from the necks, which appear to be European Orders. The objects held in left hands have been broken off. The hats are similar to that on the head of the figure, Fig. 91, Plate XV. Ground ornamented with the usual foil ornaments incised.

Fig. 16.—Bronze plaque, figure of warrior with pot helmet, button on top. Coral choker, badge of rank, on neck. Leopards' teeth necklace. Quadrangular bell on breast. Armlets, anklets, &c. Four rosettes on ground, and the usual foil ornaments incised.

Fig. 17.—Bronze plaque, figure of warrior with spear in right hand, shield in left hand; pot helmet, button on top. Quadrangular bell hanging from neck. Coral choker, badge of rank. Leopards' teeth necklace. Leopard's skin dress with head to front. On the ground are two horses' heads below and two rosettes above. Ground ornamented with the usual foil ornaments incised.

Fig. 18.—Bronze plaque, figure of warrior. Peculiarly ornamented head-dress. Coral choker, badge of rank. Leopards' teeth necklace. Broad leaf-shaped sword in right hand. Coral sash on breast. Leopard's mask hanging on left side. Armlets, anklets, &c. Small figure of boy, naked, to right, holding a metal dish with lid in form of an ox's head. A similar object may be seen amongst the Benin objects in the British Museum.

Antique Works of Art from Benin 17

DESCRIPTION OF PLATE V.

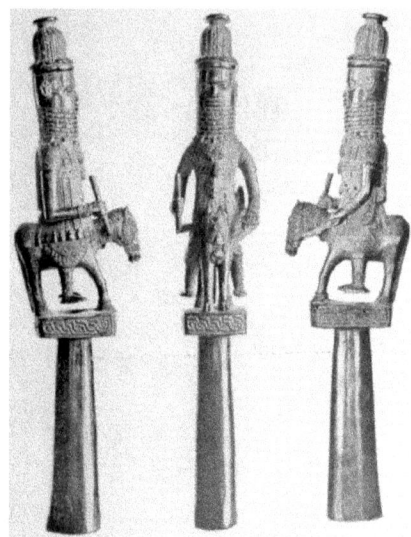

Figs. 19, 20 and 21.—Stained ivory carving of figure on horse. Coral choker; spear in right hand, the shaft broken. Tribal marks on forehead incised. Chain-bridle or head-collar. Degenerate guilloche pattern on base. Straight line diaper pattern represented in various parts. The stand formed as a socket for a pole.

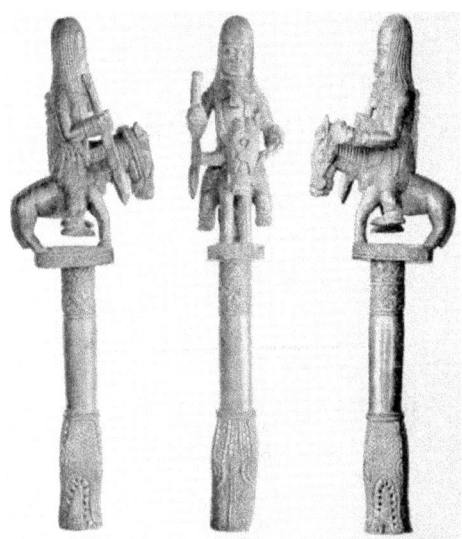

Figs. 22, 23 and 24.—Ivory carving of figure on horse, with spear in right hand and bell on neck, and long hair. The bridle formed as a head-collar. Degenerate guilloche pattern on base. The stand formed as a socket for a pole ornamented with bands of interlaced pattern and the head of an animal.

DESCRIPTION OF PLATE VI.

Figs. 25 and 26.—Ivory carving of a human face. Eyes and bands on forehead inlaid. Straight line diaper pattern on head-dress, above which are conventionalised mud-fish. Four bands of coral across forehead. Ears long and narrow. Found hidden in an oaken chest inside the sleeping apartment of King Duboar.

Fig. 27.—Carved wooden panel, consisting of a chief in the centre; broad leaf-shaped sword, with ring attached to pommel, upheld in right hand, studded with copper nails, and ornamented with representations of itself. In left hand a fan-shaped figure terminating in two hands. Coral choker, badge of rank. Bell on neck and cross-belts. Skirt ornamented with three heads and a guilloche pattern of three bands with pellets. Anklets. Attendant on left holding umbrella over chief's head. Serpent with human arm and hand in its mouth, head upwards; eyes of inlaid glass; body studded with copper nails. Leopard, drawn head upwards. On right, figure with jug in left hand and cup in right hand, standing in a trough or open vessel. Small attendant with paddle in right hand. At top a bottle bound with grass, and figure of some object, perhaps a stone celt bound with grass. Brass and iron screws are used for ornamentation in this carving. Guilloche pattern of two bands without pellets around the edge of the panel.

Figs. 28, 29 and 30.—Ivory carved tusk, 4 feet 1 inch long from bottom to point; traversed by five bands of interlaced strap-work. The other ornamentation consists of:— Human figures with hands crossed on breast; bird standing on pedestal; human figures with hands holding sashes; trees growing downwards; a rosette; mudfish; crocodiles with heads upwards; a serpent with sinuous body, head downwards; two cups; a serpent, head upwards; detached human heads. Some of the representations are so rude that it requires experience to understand their meaning. On this tusk the interlaced pattern is the prevailing ornament, and it passes into the guilloche pattern. This tusk is more tastefully decorated than the other tusk, Figs. 167 and 168, Plate XXVI, but with less variety in the carving. These carved tusks are said to represent gods in the Ju-ju houses.

DESCRIPTION OF PLATE VII.

Figs. 31 and 32.—Ivory carving of female. The design as rude as found in any part of Africa. Necklet and armlets the same as on the bronze figures.

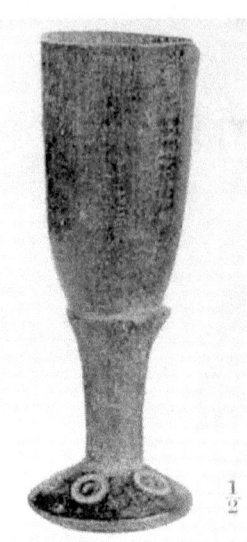

Fig. 33.—Ivory cup, stained brown.

Fig. 34.—Bronze drinking cup, the same as represented in wood-carving, Fig. 27, Plate VI.

Figs. 35 and 36.—Lion in bronze. The back is cut in a curved line, as if adapting it as a foot to some object.

Fig. 37.—Bracelet of brass, somewhat twisted.

Fig. 38.—Bracelet of brass, with five projections set with agate.

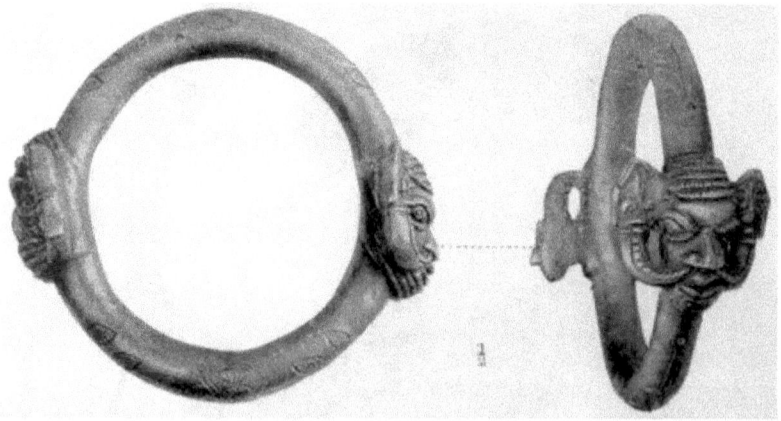

Figs. 39 and 40.—Brass bracelet, with negro heads of copper inlaid. Mud-fish springing from nose on each side and turned up. Coral chokers, badges of rank. The ring is decorated with incised floral ornaments.

DESCRIPTION OF PLATE VIII.

Figs. 41 and 42.—Figure of a warrior in bronze, with leopard's skin dress; javelins in one hand and shield in the other. Head-dress of peculiar form, with feathers. Leopards' teeth necklace. Quadrangular bell on breast.

Figs. 43 and 44.—Female figure in bronze, holding up a tablet in right hand. Head-dress, necklace, &c., of coral or agate. Three tribal marks over each eye.

Figs. 45 and 46.—Bronze vessel, somewhat in the form of a coffee-pot. Handle at back, consisting of a snake with a sinuous body, head downwards, holding a full-length human figure in its mouth. The spout consists of a human figure, seated, with two tails; and the spout springs out of the mouth between the teeth of the figure. Round the swell of the vessel are four figures resembling frogs, the bodies ornamented as human heads; nearly similar ornaments are seen on Mexican stone carvings in this collection. The four feet resemble human feet with anklets, all pointing to the front. The lid is ornamented with a human figure seated and four masks, and is fastened to the pot by a hinge.

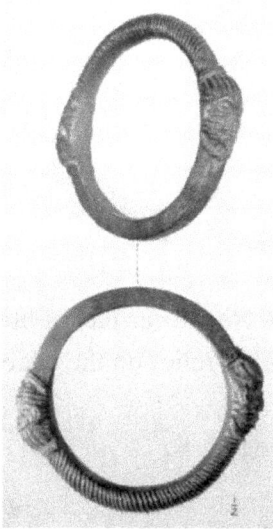

Figs. 47 and 48.—Bracelet of bronze, ornamented with two rudely formed human heads; some of the yellow earth of the mould appears to be adhering to the interstices.

Antique Works of Art from Benin **29**

DESCRIPTION OF PLATE IX.

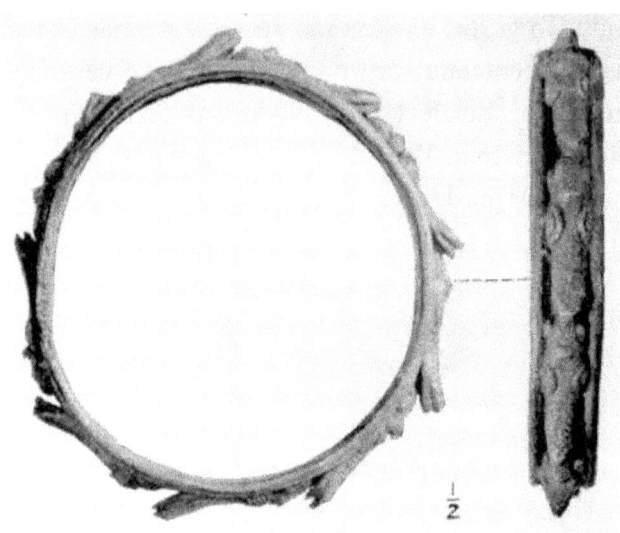

Figs. 49 and 50.—Narrow armlet of brass, with a succession of animals (? Lizards) in relief on the edge.

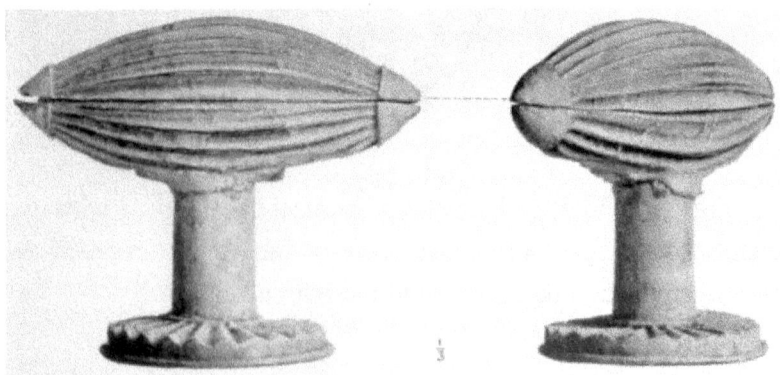

Figs. 51 and 52.—Bronze pointed dish on stand, with ribbed

cover, rabbetted. Use unknown; perhaps an European ecclesiastical utensil.

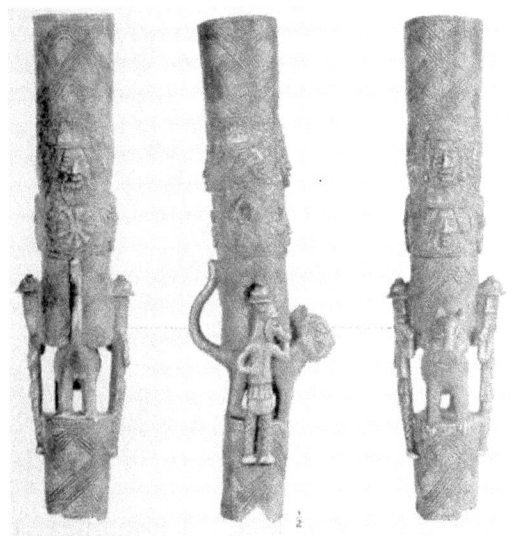

Figs. 53 to 55.—Head of a mace, ornamented with leopard and keepers and heads in bas-relief; decorated with interlaced strap-work, with brass inlaid in copper. The human heads are partly negro, whilst others from their straight hair appear to be white men, perhaps Arabs or cross-breds. The mud-fish is represented one on each side. Described by Mr. H. Ling Roth in "The Reliquary," Vol. IV, 1898, p. 162.

Figs. 56 and 57.—Bronze bottle or power flask, representing a female with barbed arrow-points extending from both sides of the mouth; perhaps symbolical; and holding a four-pronged instrument in the right hand. Three tribal marks over each eye; coral necklace.

DESCRIPTION OF PLATE X.

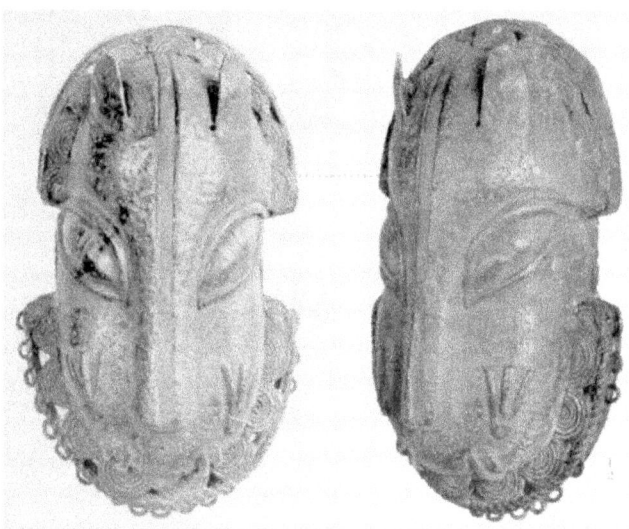

Figs. 58 and 59.—Leopard's mask head of brass, the pupils of the eyes represented by a copper band. A band of copper inlaid along the nose and forehead. A barbed figure on each cheek.

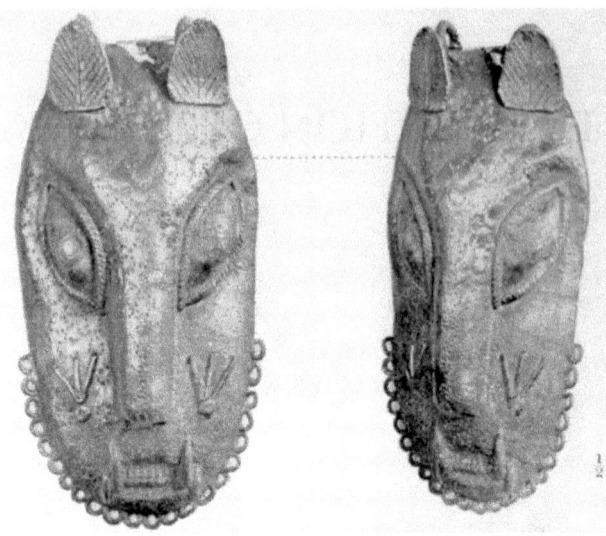

Figs. 60 and 61.—Leopard's mask head of brass, the pupils of the eyes represented by bands. A barbed figure on each cheek. Eyelets along the edges, perhaps to receive crotals as in Figs. 58 and 59.

Figs. 62 and 63.—Leopard's head in brass, the spots and pupils of eyes in copper. This appears to have been attached with a leather thong to the dress.

Figs. 64 and 65.—Bronze vase. The design appears to be purely native. It is ornamented with four human masks, two of which are ribbed. There are two elephants' heads with tusks, but no trunks over each ribbed head. Four bands of plain guilloche pattern arranged vertically between the heads. Concentric circles. Thickness of metal on unornamented parts, 2 mm.

DESCRIPTION OF PLATE XI.

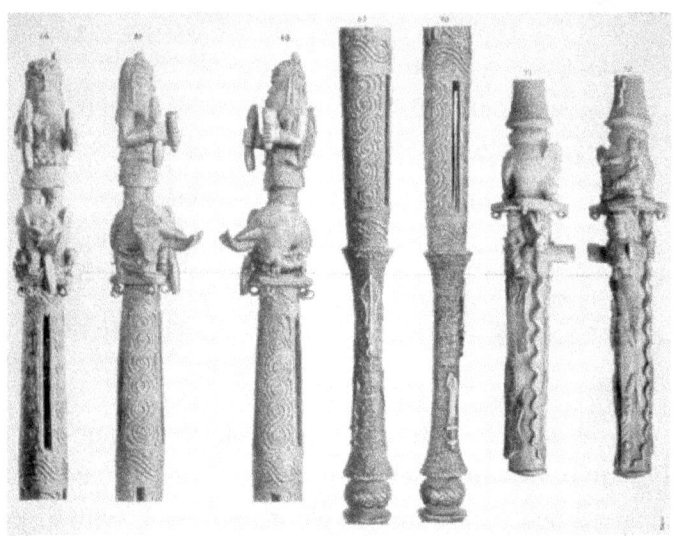

Figs. 66 to 72.—The historic mace of office of Duboar, late King of Benin; 5 feet 4 inches long, and made of brass. This was found by an officer of the expedition in the state apartment of the palaver house, and was evidently left behind by the king's people on account of its heavy weight, in their hurried exodus from Benin city; the king is said to have since recognized this staff, and stated that it had been handed down for many hundreds of years from king to king. It has the representation of "Overami," or reigning monarch, on the summit, dressed in the usual manner of Benin warriors. He is standing on an elephant which has a proboscis terminating in a human hand. This peculiarity is represented very often in the bronze antiquities of the Benin country, and especially on the carved tusk, Figs. 167 and 168, Plate XXVI, and must probably represent some great fetish; the present race, on enquiries being made, could not elucidate this matter, so its history must date back many ages. This elephant is in turn supported by the usual two royal leopards. The monarch holds in his right hand his chief ju-ju, which never leaves him night or day; in his left hand he holds a neolithic or stone axe head, edge upwards, which are looked up to by the natives even now with great awe and superstition. The interior of the upper part of the mace is hollow, having a piece of metal inside, formed like a long crotal, and was used as a bell to keep order. The broad leaf-shaped swords and the execution swords are depicted in several places over the mace. It is ornamented with guilloche pattern of two and three bands with intervening pellets. Part of the mace is ornamented in imitation of twine binding. Near the foot of the staff is the figure of another elephant with proboscis terminating in a human hand, holding a plant like a prickly-pear. Beneath the elephant are two human figures, with Maltese crosses on breasts, axes in left hands, and sticks in right. Below this are two axes hafted in serpents' heads, which have human hands in their mouths and sinuous bodies. Crocodile, head downwards, and two interlaced mud-fish.

DESCRIPTION OF PLATE XII.

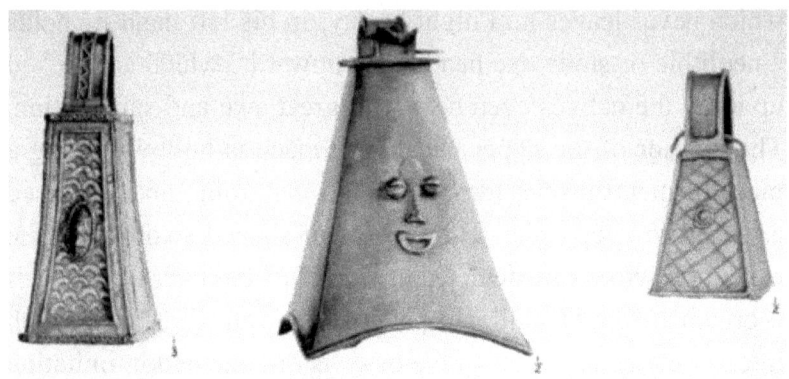

Figs. 73 to 75.—Three triangular brass bells. Fig. 73 has a negro head in relief on the front and fish-scale pattern.

Fig. 74 has the eyes, nose and mouth of a human face only.

Fig. 75 has a spiral in place of a face.

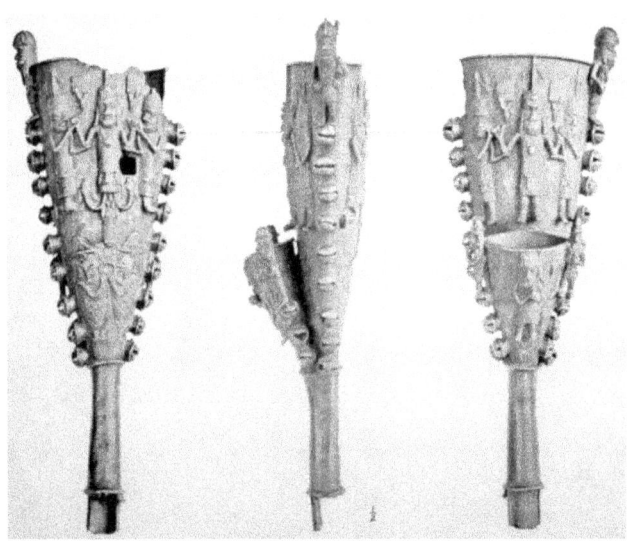

Figs. 76 to 78.—Sistrum in brass, representing two cups, the lower one ornamented with a figure holding a ball. The upper figures on each side represent a king with the arms upheld by attendants on both sides; on one side the attendants are kneeling. A hand holding a plaque or book is represented on each side. Crotals are attached to the sistrum on both sides. A stand in form of a socket to fit a pole and a band ornamented with interlaced strap-work. This object appears certainly to be a sistrum, as human figures are shown in some of the plaques holding them in their hands and striking them with a rod to produce a sound. A similar instrument in iron, modern, is figured by Mr. Ling Roth, in "The Reliquary," Vol. IV, 1898, p. 165, from the Yoruba country.

DESCRIPTION OF PLATE XIII.

Figs. 79 to 81.—Figure of a warrior on horseback. Spear in right hand, the blade having an ogee corrugated section, similar to those used in all parts of Africa where metal blades are used. The edges of the blade are bent over by rough usage, which makes it look like a spoon. The duct for the metal runs from the head of the horse. Darts in left hand. The ends of the spear and darts are bent inwards, as if by rough usage. The chain halter is similar to those seen on other horses and is used as a bridle, held by the little finger of the left hand. A circular shield, similar to the one in this collection (Plate XVIII, Fig. 102), though differently decorated, is slung on the left side over the thigh. The spurs attached to the legs have four points arranged horizontally. The figure has a leopard's skin on front and back, ornamented with representations of cowrie shells. The coat and collar bordered with interlaced strap-work. Dagger on right side. Crown, apparently of feathers, on head. Base ornamented with interlaced strap-work or guilloche pattern. The horse is fairly well formed. The hair conventionalized in straight lines. The face is that of a negro.

DESCRIPTION OF PLATE XIV.

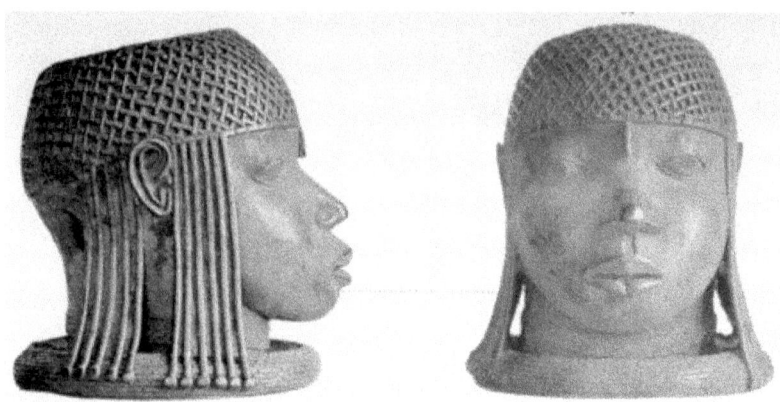

Figs. 82 and 83.—Well-formed bronze head of a negress. Reticulated head-dress of agate or coral. Coral necklace. Pendant of agate on centre of forehead. The pupils of the eyes inlaid apparently with iron. The upper lip has been inlaid probably with brass. Eleven bands of coral or agate hang from the head-dress on each side. Well-formed ears. This and Figs. 88 and 89, Plate XV, and Figs. 98 and 99, Plate XVII, are the best formed heads in the collection.

Figs. 84 and 85.—Bronze figure firing a gun, probably representing an European, with beard, presenting a flint-lock gun. The barrel of the gun is broken off at the left hand. European morion of the sixteenth century on head, ornamented with interlaced strap-work. Sword or cutlass with European guard and a flint-lock pistol slung on left side. On the right side, a dagger. Armour ornamented with strap-work or interlaced work. On the pedestal are represented two flint-lock pistols, a cross-bow, a three-pronged spear, two figures holding guns and interlaced strap-work.

DESCRIPTION OF PLATE XV.

Figs. 86 and 87.—Brass head inlaid with a copper band along the nose. The pupils of the eyes inlaid with iron. Reticulated head-dress of coral or agate. Three tribal marks over each eye. Conventionalized mud-fish in a frill around neck.

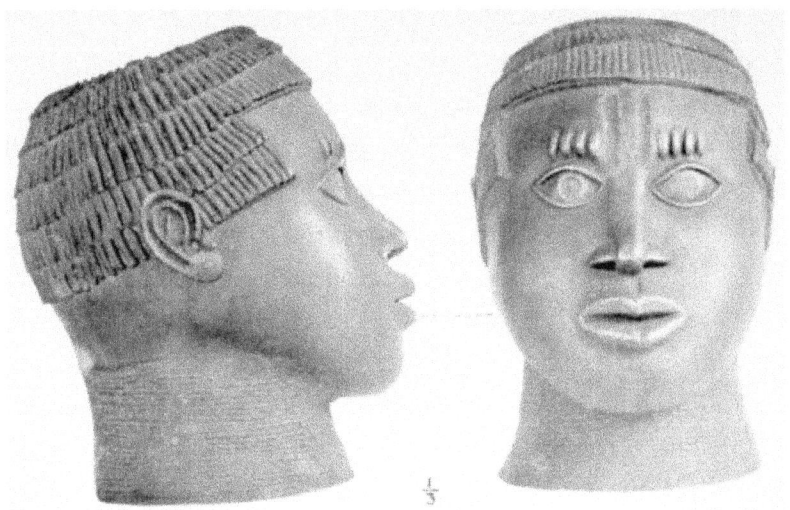

Figs. 88 and 89.—Well-formed head in bronze, the forehead decorated with two inlaid bands and four raised tribal marks over each eye. The pupils of the eyes inlaid apparently with iron. Coral necklace. The hair in conventional bands of ridges; the ears unusually well formed.

Figs. 90 and 91.—Human figure standing in bronze. Negro features. Three tribal marks over each eye. Curved lines of circles and hatchings above and below the eyes. Three radiating lines branching from the corners of the mouth. Pot helmet, with brim and reticulated ornamentation. The ears are very rudely formed. An object somewhat resembling a key or axe in the left hand. There appears to have been a staff or pole in the right hand. A cross with equal arms hangs on the breast by a chain, apparently resembling a religious order. The skirt only slightly tucked up on left side, ornamented with a guilloche pattern of two bands. A rough cast. This figure is very similar to Figs. 293 and 294, Plate XXXVIII.

Figs. 92 and 93.—Female, in bronze, with staff in left hand. Skirt ornamented with three bands of guilloche pattern. Head-dress of coral or agate. Coral choker, and tribal marks.

DESCRIPTION OF PLATE XVI.

Figs. 94 and 95.—Bronze cast of human head. Negro features. Three tribal marks over each eye. Pupils of eyes inlaid with iron. Reticulated head-dress and rosettes of coral or agate, similar to that represented in Plate XXI, Fig. 121. Coral choker, badge of rank. Twelve bands of coral and a band apparently of plaited hair hanging from head-dress on each side.

Figs. 96 and 97.—Human head in brass. Marked negro features, tattoed with dots and hatchings above and below the eyes. Branch-like figures, perhaps coral, growing out of the eyes. Three tribal marks over each eye. Pupils of eyes inlaid with iron. Reticulated head-dress and rosettes, of coral or agate, similar to those represented in Plate XXI, Fig. 121. Peculiar figures on each side of the head-dress, perhaps representing feathers. Coral choker, badge of rank. Bands of coral or agate hang down from the head-dress at the sides and back of the head. On the projecting base are represented two leopards, an ox's head, and other animals, four arms and hands, and a neolithic celt in front.

DESCRIPTION OF PLATE XVII.

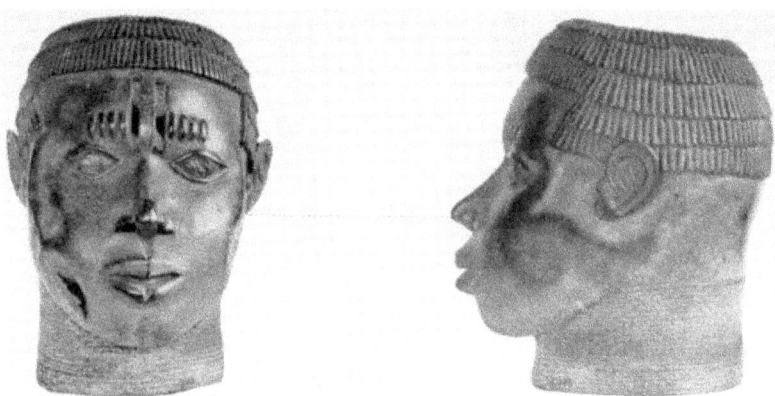

Figs. 98 and 99.—Well-formed head in bronze, the forehead decorated with two inlaid bands and four raised cicatrices (tribal marks) over each eye. The pupils of the eyes inlaid apparently with iron, coral necklace, a badge of rank. The metal is very thin, being only 1 mm. in thickness. The hair in conventional bands of ridges; the ears unusually well formed.

Figs. 100 and 101.—Bronze cast of human head. Marked negro features, rudely formed. Three tribal marks over each eye. Peculiar pointed reticulated head-dress of coral or agate. Curious lines of incised circles above and below the eyes. Coral choker, badge of rank. Bands of coral or agate hanging down on both sides and at the back. Ears badly formed. The projecting base ornamented with a guilloche pattern of two bands with pellets.

DESCRIPTION OF PLATE XVIII.

Fig. 102.—Brass shield, 2 feet in diameter and ·08 inch in thickness, ornamented with three concentric rings. The outer one represents a row of leopards, with human heads and head-dresses alternating. A broad leaf-shaped sword, similar to Fig. 106, and two execution swords, similar to Fig. 110, are also represented on this ring. The middle ring is ornamented with a serpent with sinuous body, having its tail in its mouth. The inner ring is filled with foil ornaments, and small circles cover both this and the outer ring. There is a square hole in the centre for the attachment of the handle. The shield resembles that slung on the left hip of the mounted warrior, Figs. 79 to 81, Plate XIII, but with different ornamentation.

Antique Works of Art from Benin 51

Fig. 103.—Iron dart, or spear, 5 feet 1 inch long, with wooden shaft. The blade is leaf-shaped with socket, and is rudely forged.

Fig. 104.—Iron dart, 3 feet 7¼ inches long, with barbed head and iron shaft.

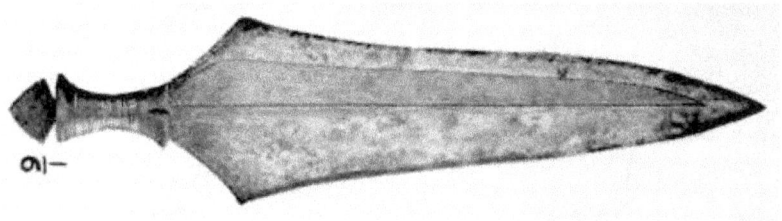

Fig. 105.—Iron dagger, or short sword, length 16¼ inches; the incised ornamentation is on alternate sides, like those of the Gaboon and other parts of Africa. There are also sinuous lines engraved on alternate sides. It is rudely forged, and the handle is very small and bound with strips of copper.

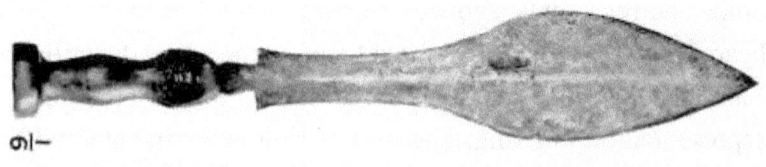

Fig. 106.—Iron leaf-shaped sword, length 19¼ inches, similar in form to those frequently represented in the hands of warriors on the plaques. It is rudely forged. The wooden handle is inlaid with copper.

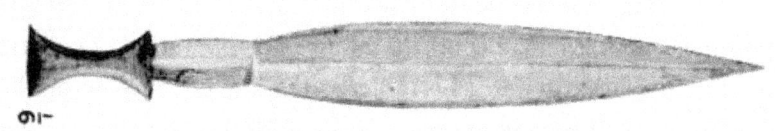

Fig. 107.—Iron leaf-shaped sword, length 19½ inches, with alternating ornamentation on the opposite sides of the blade, similar to that prevailing in the Gaboon and other parts of Africa. The handle is very small, and is bound with strips of iron.

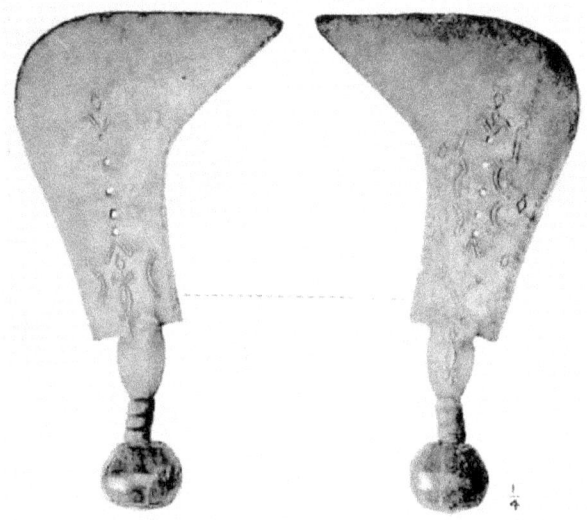

Figs. 108 and 109.—Brass implement, resembling a bill-hook. The edge is on the convex side and the concave side is blunt. It is pierced with five holes and engraved with hatchings in Benin style, in which are included two stars, a cross, and three crocodiles.

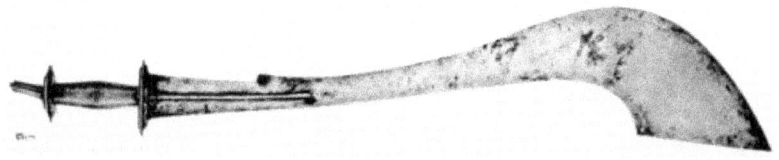

Fig. 110.—Iron execution sword, 3 feet 1 inch long, hilt and pommel of brass, with copper inlaid ornamentation. The grip bound with brass wire. It is single-edged, the edge being on the convex side. It resembles the swords engraved on the circular shield, Fig. 102, one on each side of the broad leaf-shaped sword. This kind of sword is held in the hands of warriors on two plaques in this collection, Fig. 254, Plate XXXIII, and Fig. 291, Plate XXXVIII. It is also seen on the carved cocoa-nut, Fig. 220, Plate XXX, and elsewhere. It is rudely forged.

DESCRIPTION OF PLATE XIX.

Fig. 111.—Bronze ægis, representing a chief standing with attendants holding up his hands in a manner similar to Figs. 76-78, Plate XII, and Figs. 167 and 168, Plate XXVIII. Frogs between the feet. Cylindrical spikes on head-dresses.

Fig. 112.—Bronze ægis, representing man on horseback to left, wearing single-edged sword with guard. A ranseur of the sixteenth or seventeenth century in right hand, point down. The hair is straight and combed out, and may probably represent a white man. The chain bridle is held up in left hand. Small crotals with chains hang from the eyelets on the edge of the ægis. Pattern of fish-scales on ground similar to that on the brass bell, Fig. 73, Plate XII, and elsewhere.

Figs. 113 and 114.—Bronze plaque, representing a figure standing; long spear, multibarbed, with ogee-sectioned blade in right hand, pointing downwards, knob at butt end. There are twelve ducts running from the ground of the plaque to the shaft of the spear. In left hand a broad leaf-shaped sword, with a ring attached to pommel, like Figs. 4, 13, 114, 131, 254, 255, &c. Dress like a nightshirt, and composed apparently of strings of coral, with bare arms. Dagger or short sword on left side. Quadrangular bell on neck; teeth necklace; coral choker, badge of rank. Head-dress of metal, in form somewhat resembling a grenadier cap. Six rosettes on ground, and quatrefoil leaves incised.

DESCRIPTION OF PLATE XX.

Fig. 115.—Brass key, a good deal filed and tooled all over. Handle ornamented with twisted rope pattern. The form of this key cannot be identified as Roman, and is probably European.

Fig. 116.—Bronze stand for the game of mancala, with ten holes and two irregular-shaped cavities in the centre. It is the same game as Figs. 184 and 185, Plate XXVIII, but with fewer holes. The sides are ornamented with interlaced strap-work, and the stem and the edge of the base with varieties of guilloche pattern. This game is distributed nearly all over Africa, and is said to be found wherever Arab influence is seen. It is also found in Palestine, Syria, Arabia, Maldive Islands, India, Ceylon, Malay Peninsula, Java, and the Philippine Islands.

Fig. 117.—Brass bell, with reticulated pierced work. Negro head on front. This bell is interesting as being a survival of the bells so often seen hanging from the necks of the figures on the plaques. It is evident that it never could have emitted any sound.

Fig. 118.—Entire tortoise shell, upper and under sides, in brass; ornamented on the upper side with geometrical pattern; each figure inlaid with a copper bolt or stud in the centre.

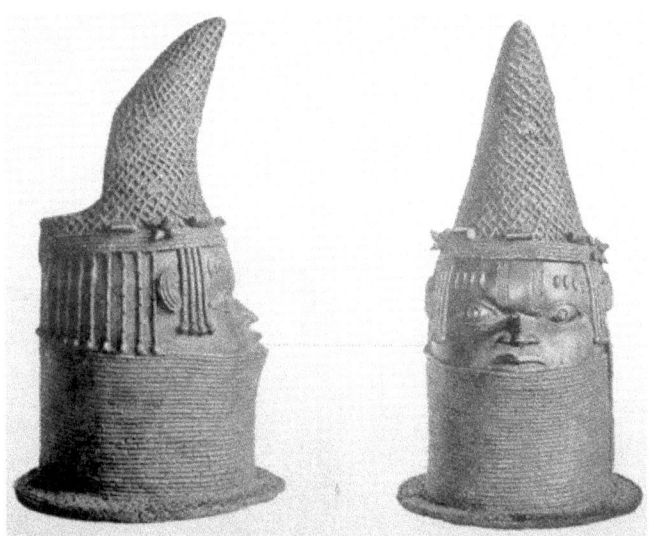

Figs. 119 and 120.—Bronze human head for holding carved elephants' tusks. The head-dress, pointed and reticulated, representing coral or agate. Four tribal marks over each eye. Six vertical bands of inlaid iron-work over the nose. The pupils of the eyes are of iron. The head-dress resembles Figs. 100 and 101, Plate XVII. Coral choker. Guilloche pattern on projecting base.

DESCRIPTION OF PLATE XXI.

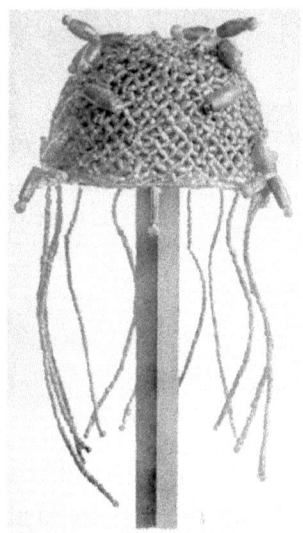

Fig. 121.—Head-dress composed entirely of agate. It serves to explain the construction of the head-dresses on the bronze plaques and figures, showing how the reticulated effect on the plaques is formed by beads of agate strung together in a kind of network. The rosettes of agate, and the tags and pendants are also explained by this figure. See Figs. 2, 4, 43, 44, 82, 83, 86, 87, 94, 95, 96, 97, 100, 101, 119, 120, 124, 125, 126, 127, 232-234, 277, 278, &c.

Figs. 122 and 123.—Circular brass box, ornamented on the top with a central figure in repoussé work, holding two crocodiles upright in each hand. The legs terminate in a band turned up on each side as shown in other designs in Benin art. There are also circular heads having tribal marks over the eyes. Rosettes, guilloche and fish-scale patterns are also represented in repoussé. The pieces of the box are rivetted together with bands of copper. This appears to be the kind of box represented in the hands of one of the smaller figures in the plaque, Fig. 179, Plate XXVII. The latter, however, is taller. These objects have been described by Mr. C. Read as drums in his paper in the "Journ. Anthrop. Inst.," Vol. XXVII, Plate XVIII, Fig. 4. Viewed as a drum, the projecting flanges at top and bottom are not explained.

Figs. 124 and 125.—Human mask of brass; the pupils of the eyes inlaid with iron. Reticulated head-dress, with rosettes probably of agate. Three tribal marks over each eye. Rows of semi-circles filled with semi-circles round neck. The features are rounded, and, although a good deal tooled, are less flattened by filing than some of these masks. This is a good specimen of Benin art.

Figs. 126 and 127.—Human mask of brass; the pupils of the eyes inlaid with iron. Reticulated head-dress, with rosettes probably of agate. Coral band above the forehead. Three tribal marks over each eye. Ears badly formed. Coral choker, badge of rank. Guilloche pattern, with pellets round neck. The face is very much tooled and filed, and the lips and nose flattened by filing. Crotals have probably been suspended from the eyelets below, as indicated by the eight links of chains left remaining (see Plate XIX, Fig. 112).

DESCRIPTION OF PLATE XXII.

Fig. 128.—Armlet entirely of brass, without other metal. Ornamented with four upright figures and four horizontal heads. The upright figures have their forearms elevated. The legs are very attenuated and the skirt of the dress very pronounced. Eyebrows extremely prominent, and the head-dress of peculiar form and conical. The armlet is surmounted by raised bands, which pass over the figures, and are separated by pierced work. Broad rims are shown at top and bottom, and are edged with herring-bone pattern.

Fig. 129.—Bronze plaque, representing human figure with beard, riding to right; a ranseur of the sixteenth or seventeenth century in right hand, point downwards. Hair combed out straight. No tribal marks. Bodice fastened with buttons. Pleated kilt like Figs. 235 and 236, Plate XXXI, and Fig. 247, Plate XXXII. Twisted or plaited bridle of some limp substance in left hand. Bell and crotals on horse's neck. Leopards in relief behind figure of horse. Ground ornamented with trefoil leaves and punch-marks. This figure does not appear to be negro. The horse appears to be galloping, which is not the usual Benin method of locomotion.

Fig. 130.—Bronze plaque, representing two warriors with long, narrow, leaf-shaped swords upheld in right hands. Peculiar head-dress, a broad band on the frontal. Hair parted in the middle and hanging down behind. One figure has a beard. Both have objects resembling bows slung upon left arm. Leopards' teeth necklaces and quadrangular bells hanging from necks. Ground ornamented with leaf-shaped foil ornaments incised.

Fig. 131.—Bronze plaque, representing five figures; central figure holding a staff of unusual form in right hand; coral choker; oval head-dress; small bells attached to straps hanging down from girdle; anklets and armlets, the former adorned with crotals; left hand on handle of sword in scabbard on left side. Small figures on each side with javelins, the points in a sheath. The larger attendants on each side holding shields over the central figure, as described by De Bry in the seventeenth century. All the attendants have a bag on right side, strapped over shoulder. One of the smaller attendants has a broad leaf-shaped sword upheld in right hand, holding it by the ring attached to the pommel.

DESCRIPTION OF PLATE XXIII.

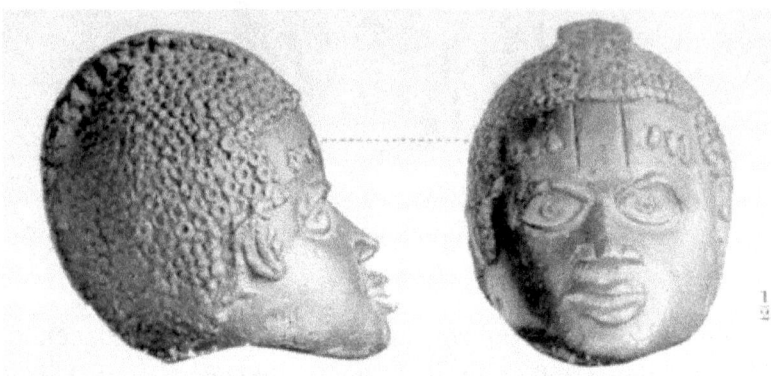

Figs. 132 and 133.—Small head of boy, in bronze, with three raised tribal marks over each eye, and two vertical marks on forehead. Head-dress with crest.

Fig. 134.—Figures in bronze, representing two rude human figures, male and female, attending an animal, probably a bear. A plate, or board, of three rows of circles with ten circles in each row, is laid out before the figures, and is perhaps a game of mancala, of which examples are seen in Plate XX, Fig. 116, and Plate XXVIII, Figs. 184 and 185. The female figure has very large anklets, and her hands are spread upon her stomach. The hair is plaited and ornamented with knobs, resembling a Mexican pottery figure in this collection. The hair of the male figure is plaited and turned over on the left side, and he is sitting cross-legged. His left arm and hand are spread upon the bear, and he has a rod in the right hand. A burnt core of sand is seen under the thin metal pedestal.

Fig. 135.—Brass bottle, hung by chain, and ornamented with representation of twisted twine, and a guilloche pattern without pellets round the swell. The rings for hanging it are similar to

those on the powder flask, Figs. 56 and 57, Plate IX. A similar brass bottle, but smaller, is represented in Plate XXXV, Fig. 267.

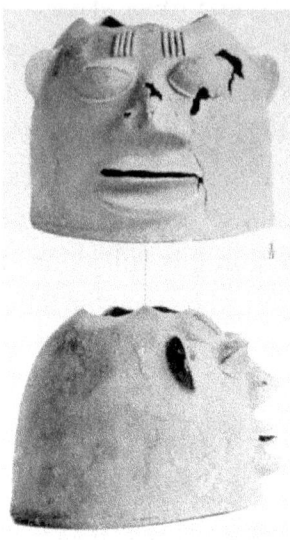

Figs. 137 and 138.—A very rude head of bronze; probably used as the stand for a carved tusk. Four tribal marks over each eye; the eyes projecting like those of Figs. 265-6, Plate 35. This is the rudest head in the collection.

Fig. 139.—A cylindrical stand of bronze, for carved tusks, representing on the outside four female figures standing, with bands of upright interlaced strap-work between. All the figures are holding objects in their hands. One holds a bird, another a sistrum, which is being beaten with a stick; the rest are broken. Two of the bands of interlaced strap-work are of thin repoussé work, and nailed on with bronze nails. The base and top are ornamented with looped straps, similar to No. 140. All the figures have three incised tribal marks over the eyes, and crested head-gear. A vertical hole for the carved tusk runs down the centre, like those in all the human heads.

Fig. 140.—Armlet of brass, pierced work, ornamented with bands of looped straps, similar to Fig. 139, and two bands of concentric semicircles alternating with Maltese crosses. Around the centre is a band of broken guilloche pattern, forming a transitional link between the guilloche, and a peculiar floral ornament common to Benin art. The representation of European

screw-heads forms part of the ornamentation, and raised eyelets alternate with the screw-head ornaments.

Fig. 141.—Armlet of copper, ornamented with horizontal human heads of brass. The head-dresses are ornamented with fish-scale pattern, and the hair is combed out straight. The heads alternate with double-coiled mud-fish, resembling Fig. 276, Plate XXXVI. It is not quite easy to understand how this work was done. Both the copper and the brass appear to have been formed by casting.

DESCRIPTION OF PLATE XXIV.

Fig. 142.—Bronze open-mouthed vessel, with six projecting eyelets round the neck, and a handle.

Figs. 143 and 144.—Bronze or brass figure of cock, 22 inches high, including pedestal. The feathers are represented in straight and curved lines of hatchings. The pupils of the eyes are inlaid copper, of lozenge-shaped form. The tarsus is unnaturally broad. On the top of the pedestal in front is a Maltese cross, with a band of interlaced strap-work. The sides of the base are ornamented with interlaced strap-work, and representations of three ox's heads are on the front. A fine specimen of barbaric art.

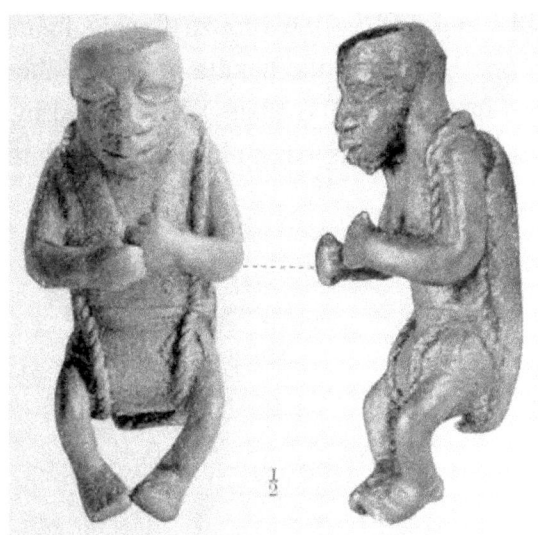

Figs. 145 and 146.—Human naked figure of bronze. A large thick plaster covers the whole of the back, and is fastened on with cords round the arms and legs. Mr. H. Ling Roth believes this to represent a cure for cretinism, and says that two larger figures like it have been seen in Benin city. ("Reliquary," Vol. IV, 1898, p. 173.)

Figs. 147 and 148.—Two bronze female figures back to back, with one hat, being the handle of one of the swords or wands (see Figs. 202 to 211, Plate XXIX), used by virgins in their dances. There is a large iron pin right through the casting.

Figs. 149 and 150.—Bronze head of girl. Three tribal marks incised over each eye; pupils of eyes of iron, inlaid; necklace of agate or coral.

Figs. 151 and 152.—Brass vessel, resembling a coffee pot. A human figure sitting in front, out of the mouth of which the spout emerges. The handle at back represents a sinuous snake with the head downwards, like that of Fig. 46, Plate VIII. Bands of fish-scale pattern surround the vessel.

Antique Works of Art from Benin **79**

DESCRIPTION OF PLATE XXV.

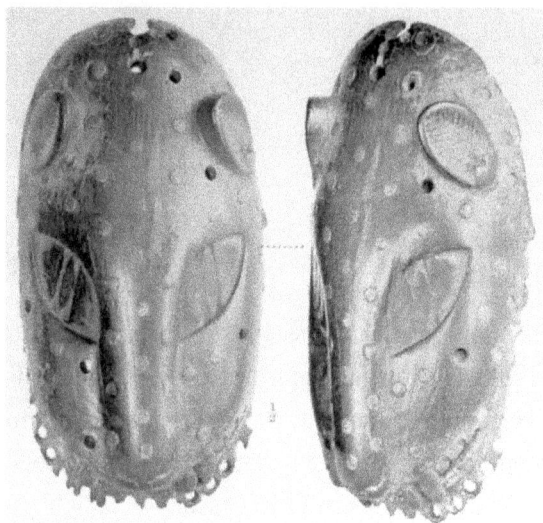

Figs. 153 and 154.—Carved ivory head of leopard, the spots of lead, inlaid. This resembles in form the bronze ones, Figs. 58-63, Plate X. It is apparently very old.

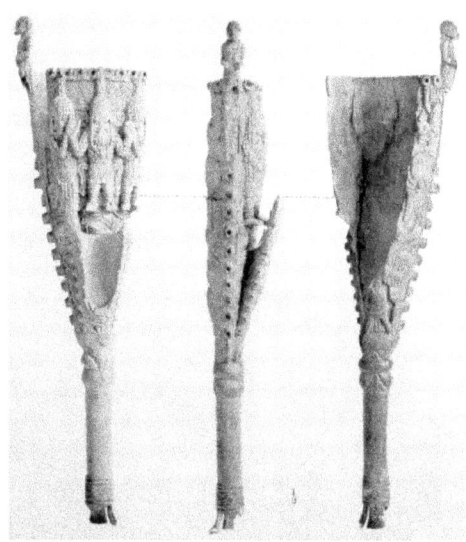

Figs. 155 to 157.—Ivory carved sistrum, with a large and a small bell, similar to the brass one, Figs. 76-78, Plate XII. On the side of the large bell is a chief standing with his hands upheld by attendants in the usual manner; a snake-headed sash hangs from waist. On the top two carved figures, one of which has been broken off. At the back of the small bell is a band of straight line diaper pattern, and on the top a crocodile's head holding a closed human hand. It is much broken. This object is of interest as showing it to be a survival derived from a metal sistrum. Mr. H. Ling Roth has described this object at some length in "The Studio," December, 1898.

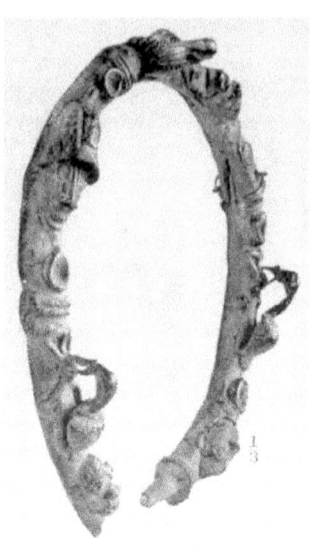

Fig. 158.—Necklace of bronze, ornamented with human heads in relief, and birds with long beaks, perhaps meant for vultures, but too long-necked for that bird, picking at the figures of extended skeletons. In the intervals between the other figures are oval holes with raised edges, probably a degenerate representation of the coiled mud-fish so frequently shown in other Benin antiquities. The fastening end of the necklace is broken, disclosing the fact that the core of the object is of some lighter material encased in copper or bronze. It has a hinge on one side, probably to facilitate the opening of it.

Figs. 159 and 160.—Brass handle of iron sword, with fragment of the iron sword in it. It has two human faces back to back, covered by one hat, as in Figs. 147 and 148, Plate XXIV, and representations of European screw-heads used as ornaments, as in Fig. 140, Plate XXIII.

Antique Works of Art from Benin **83**

Figs. 161 to 163.—Bronze staff of office, 4 feet 11 inches in length, weighing 14 lbs.; it has two elongated crotals in the upper end, with long slits for the emission of the sound, enclosing loose rods of iron. Between the slits are vertical bands of guilloche pattern with raised edges, similar to those represented on the stem and top of the mancala board, Fig. 116, Plate XX, and a horizontal band of guilloche pattern with pellets in relief. On the top is an upright human hand, holding a curled mud-fish. The middle of the staff is ornamented by curious nondescript figures alternating with balls, and the lower end has an oblong butt ornamented on the four sides with guilloche pattern, like that of the crotals on the upper end. The staff has been broken in the middle and mended by recasting in a clumsy way, the metal of the part introduced being thicker than the staff itself.

DESCRIPTION OF PLATE XXVI.

Figs. 164 and 165.—Carved ivory figure of a woman (?) standing, the arms deficient; They were fitted into square sockets on each side, and were fastened by large bronze nails, one of which remains. A row of five leopards' heads hanging from the waist-belt, edged with rows of pellets, or perhaps eyelets, but much defaced. The lips are very thick and the nose broad. The pupils of the eyes are represented by deep circular cavities. No tribal marks apparent, the breasts are not large, but pendant. The whole of the ivory is very much weathered and pitted, especially the legs and base. The figure was accompanied by another of the same size exactly like it and without arms, which was not purchased.

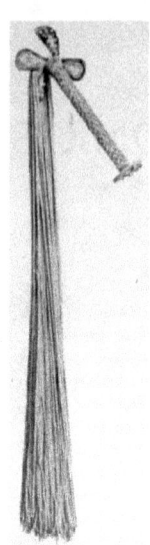

Fig. 166.—Coral whip or whisk, probably a badge of office. Four tags, two of which are ornamented with crocodiles embroidered with metal.

Figs. 167 and 168.—Ivory carved tusk, 3 feet 6 inches long

from bottom to point. Band at bottom with reticulated or square-shaped ornament, probably derived from interlacing bands. Commencing from the bottom, the ornamentation consists of:—A coiled serpent, tail in mouth. Leopard's head and human head. Human figures standing, one having a cross on breast, and a key or axe-shaped object in left hand similar to the bronze figure, Figs. 90 and 91, Plate XV; staff in right hand. Figure holding sash round waist. Elephant's head with tusks, proboscis terminating in a human hand. Human figure with spear in left hand, shield in right hand. Bird standing on pedestal. Human figure upholding broad leaf-shaped sword in right hand; bell on neck; pedestal on top of head; feather in cap. Human figure.

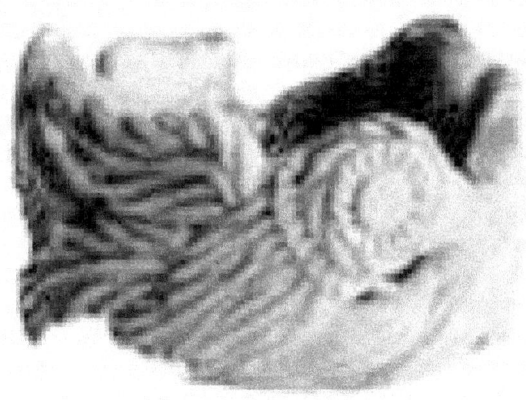

Fig. 169.—Ivory ring, carved, with 3 birds.

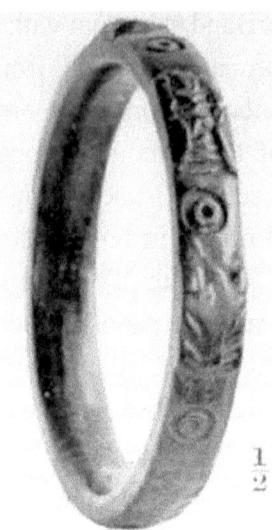

Fig. 170.—Ivory bracelet, rudely carved, with representations of leopards' and elephants' heads and perhaps the vestiges of the mud-fish.

Fig. 171.—Carved ivory bracelet, representing a snake, the eyes inlaid.

Figs. 172 and 173.—Ivory bell, or rattle. With clapper of ivory, consisting of an elephant's tusk point, with human head carved; tribal marks over eyes.

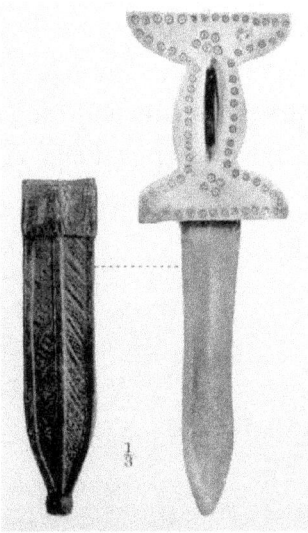

Figs. 174 and 175.—Dagger, the handle ornamented with

lines of dots and circles. The blade has an ogee section, similar to that which prevails in the Gaboon and nearly all parts of Africa.

Figs. 176 and 177.—Wooden head-dress. The horizontal bar appears to represent a shark with mouth and tail, ornamented with carved representations of animals and masks. Said to be from Benin, West Africa. The masks are quite characteristic of Benin art. The eyes of the large mask are formed of the metal bases of cartridges, which proves it to be quite modern. It is similar in character to Fig. 183, Plate XXVII. It is perhaps Jekri, see a paper by Messrs. Granville and Ling Roth in the "Journ. Anthrop. Inst.," Vol. I, New Series, Plate VIII, Fig. 3.

DESCRIPTION OF PLATE XXVII.

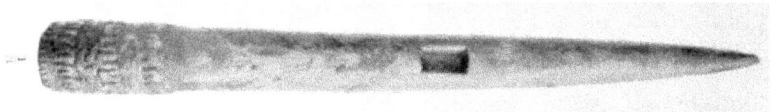

Fig. 178.—Ivory trumpet, made of the point of an elephant's tusk. Mouth-hole on the convex side. The butt end is ornamented with two snakes in two bands, tails in mouths.

Fig. 179.—Bronze plaque, with five figures; the central figure with coral choker, badge of rank, coral or agate head-dress with feather, and sash. Broad leaf-shaped sword upheld in right hand; spear, point down, in left. Two boys, one with ivory trumpet, the other holding a brass box nearly similar to Figs. 122 and 123,

Plate XXI. These objects have been described by Messrs. Read and Dalton as drums in their paper in the "Journ. Anthrop. Inst.," Vol. XXVII, Plate XVIII, Fig. 4. Viewed as a drum, the projecting flanges at top and bottom are not explained. Leopard's head on girdle. Attendants carrying shields; quadrangular bells on necks. The left attendant is holding the same spear as the central figure, point down, as in Fig. 17, Plate IV. Head-dresses of attendants with ornaments of cowrie shells. Ground ornamented with leaf-shaped foil ornaments incised.

Fig. 180.—Bronze plaque, representing the figure of a warrior, with unusually formed helmet, apparently of metal. Quadrangular bell on neck and teeth necklace. Shield on right arm, and spear with square cap at butt end, point downwards, in left hand. The ground is ornamented with two half-moons and the usual leaf-shaped foil ornaments incised.

Fig. 181.—Bronze plaque, representing three figures, the central one beating a drum with his fingers, and no drum-sticks. The drum has pegs with knobs to fasten down the skin, like Fig. 248, Plate XXXII, and similar to the Jekri drum figured in the "Journ. Anthrop. Inst.," Vol. I, New Series, Plate VIII, Fig. 5. Quadrangular bell on chest. Both the side figures hold sistri with two bells, like Figs. 76 to 78, Plate XII, upheld in their left hands, which they are beating with sticks in their right hands. This plaque gives a fair idea of the kind of music used in Benin.

Fig. 182.—Brass oblong box, lid deficient. Lock of European form and ornamentation. Faces and sides of box ornamented with raised rosettes and incised floral designs resembling that on Figs. 76 to 78, Plate XII, Fig. 225, Plate XXX, Fig. 282, Plate XXXVII, and Fig. 306, Plate XL. It has four legs, and is European in appearance.

Fig. 183.—Wooden head-dress, with carved representations of animals on top. Said to be from Benin, West Africa. It was brought over from West Africa with things from Benin. It

is similar in character to Figs. 176 and 177, Plate XXVI. It is perhaps Jekri, see a paper by Messrs. Granville and Ling Roth in the "Journ. Anthrop. Inst." Vol. I, New Series, Plate VIII, Fig. 3.

DESCRIPTION OF PLATE XXVIII.

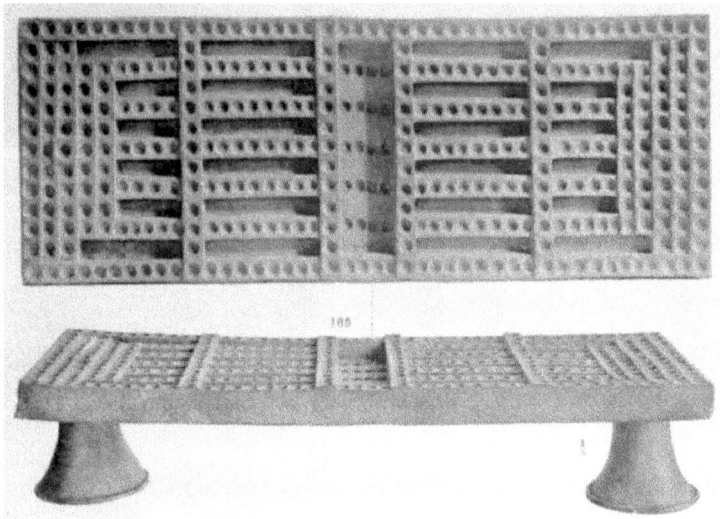

Figs. 184 and 185.—Large mancala board of bronze. It has 352 holes; another in this collection, Fig. 116, Plate XX, has only ten circular holes. The sides are ornamented with rectangular forms linked together. This game is distributed all over Africa, especially where Arab influence is seen. It is also found in Palestine, Syria, Arabia, Maldive Islands, India, Ceylon, Malay Peninsula, Java and the Philippine Islands.

Figs. 186 and 187.—Curved iron knife, with handle carved as a human figure. The edge is on the convex side.

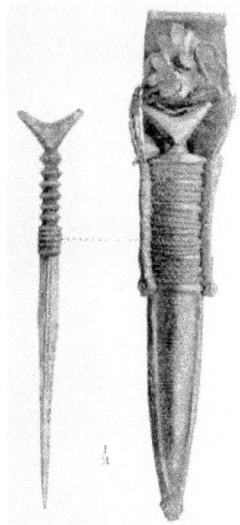

Figs. 188 and 189.—Dagger in leather sheath. Blade with a quadrilateral section. Brass handle with forked pommel.

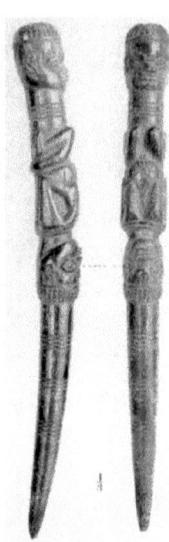

Figs. 190 and 191.—A dagger or prod of ivory. Negro head on the upper part, below which is a human female figure reversed and crouched; the hands holding the breasts; the legs crouched up. Stained yellow; blunt pointed.

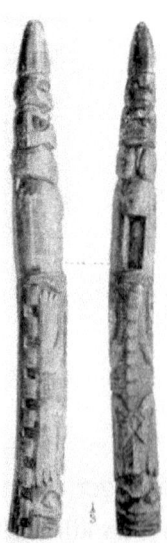

Figs. 192 and 193.—Point of elephant's tusk, carved with a representation of a human figure kneeling. At point, a skeleton of a crocodile, and a human head at base, the mouth of which is peculiar. It appears to be a whistle or musical instrument.

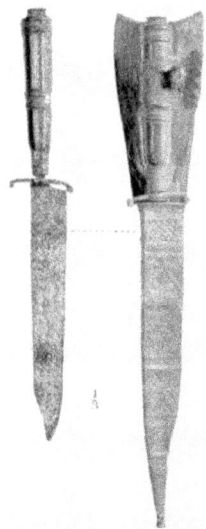

Figs. 194 and 195.—Knife with ivory handle. The brass sheath ornamented with human figures, a floral ornament, and a man on a horse.

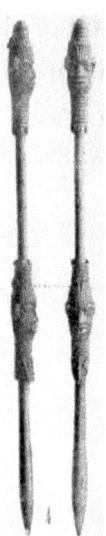

Figs. 196 and 197.—Pointed rod of bronze, ornamented with two heads. Head-dress of upper head ornamented with bands of straight line diaper pattern. Crocodile head holding lower part of the rod in mouth.

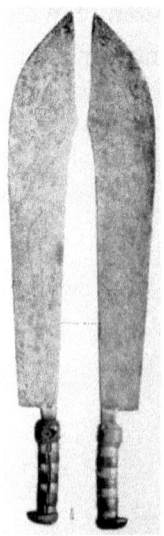

Figs. 198 and 199.—Broad knife-shaped sword of iron; the wooden handle bound with brass and iron bands alternating. On one side the blade is engraved with a human figure and an execution sword traced in lines of dots and incised lines, as is frequently the case in Australian representations of figures on wood. The other side of the blade has an ornamentation in leaves on a sinuous stem, and a square pattern of interlaced bands.

Fig. 200.—Brass bracelet, having amongst other ornaments a band of straight line diaper pattern.

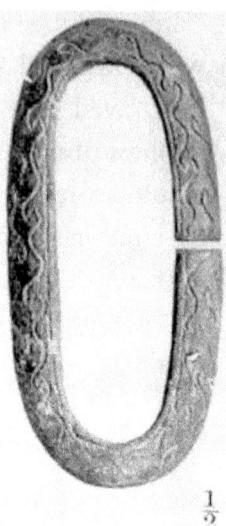

Fig. 201.—Bronze link or buckle, or portion of one, with incised floral guilloche ornament, similar to that on the brass wand, Fig. 211, Plate XXIX, and the armlets, Fig. 140, Plate XXIII, and Fig. 238, Plate XXXII.

DESCRIPTION OF PLATE XXIX.

Figs. 202 and 203.—Brass dancing sword or wand, said to be used by virgins in their dances. The handle is ornamented with two figures, which appear to be holding some objects. The blade is engraved with guilloche pattern on both sides.

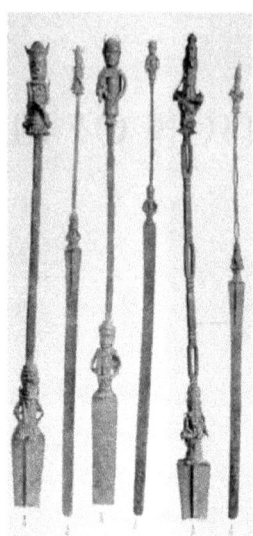

Figs. 204 to 209.—Three brass dancing swords or wands, said to be used by virgins in their dances. Each handle is ornamented by four rudely cast figures back to back, carrying objects in their hands, two of which can be identified as birds, and two or three have leaf-shaped swords with ring on pommel. One has bands of straight line diaper pattern. The blades are ornamented with guilloche patterns and floral ornaments incised.

Figs. 210 and 211.—Brass dancing sword or wand, said to be used by virgins in their dances. The handle is ornamented with four figures, which are in pairs back to back. They appear to be holding swords and other objects. The blade is ornamented on one side with bands of strap-work, and on the other with a sinuous line of branching leaves (floral guilloche). Straight line diaper pattern and lines of half-circles are on the square stem of the handle.

Figs. 212 and 213.—Iron wedge-shaped sword, single-edged, enlarging to a broad end. Ivory handle; the grip carved in pointed leaves and studded with lead; pommel in form of a leopard's head; the eyes inlaid with lead; a band carved as two scaly snakes at bottom. The scabbard worked in green plush and red cloth, with human figures and tortoises alternating. This is probably the kind of work represented in metal on some of the dresses on the plaques. The sword belts terminate in tassels of worsted or some other limp material.

Fig. 214.—Iron spear-head, modern, with ogee section, similar to those of Benin. Iron and brass bound shaft.

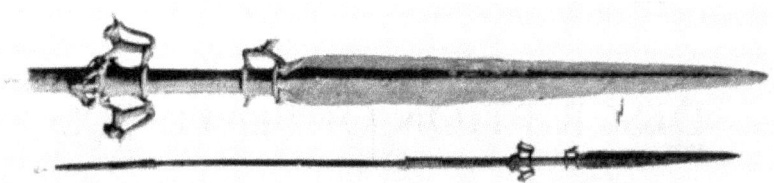

Figs. 215 and 216.—Iron spear, length 4 feet 11 inches, the head having an ogee section, similar to those used at the present time on the Gaboon and elsewhere in West Africa. Below the spear-head the shaft is ornamented with bronze figures of leopards in two places and two degenerate elephants' heads and eyes, the proboscis terminating in a human hand holding a leaf, as so frequently shown elsewhere. The butt end is cased and bound with brass. The shaft is of iron, with a brass band on the upper parts.

DESCRIPTION OF PLATE XXX.

Figs. 217 and 218.—Carved cocoa-nut, with carving representing a European in boat with spear in right hand and apparently a paddle in the left hand. Figure armed with hoe, and another cutting a palm-tree, with a kind of chisel in the right hand and a bill-hook in the left. One of the figures has distinct buttons on the coat.

Figs. 219 to 221.—Carved cocoa-nut, representing a native on a horse to left, holding up chain-bridle in left hand; spear in right hand, point down. Horse very ill-formed and indistinct. Another carving represents a figure, apparently in boat, holding spears point down. One of the figures is beating a pressure drum, which Mr. Ling Roth describes as being similar to those of the modern Yorubas. The drum-sticks used by two of the figures have curved heads and flat ends. A band of chevrons within chevrons are on the trousers of two figures. The marks on the faces consist of three lines radiating from the corners of the mouth, as in Figs. 90 and 91, Plate XV, and crosses on the cheeks. Tribal marks on faces. A native execution sword, similar to Fig. 110, Plate XVIII, and a flint-lock gun are represented separately between the other figures. The cocoa-nut is hung by a chain of European manufacture. The stopper represents a human face on two supports. Mr. H. Ling Roth, in whose possession this object formerly was, gives a more detailed account of it in "The Studio," December, 1898.

Fig. 222.—Small brass crotals with semicircular ornaments.

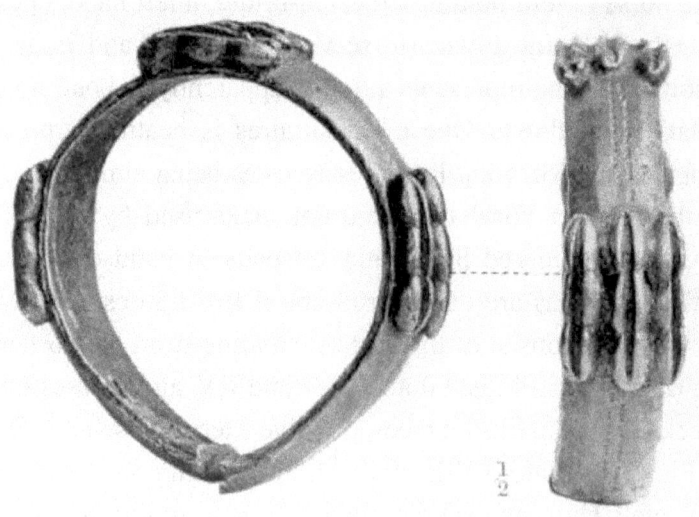

Figs. 223 and 224.—Brass bracelet, ornamented with brass representations of rows of cowrie shells, in groups of nine.

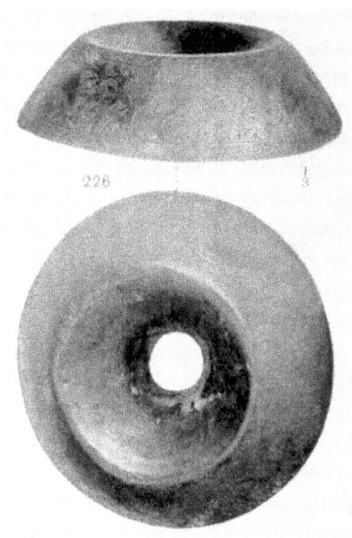

Figs. 225 and 226.—Brass object of unknown use, ornamented on the outside with three half-moons and a floral pattern in incised lines, similar to that on the brass sistrum, Figs. 76 to 78, Plate XII; the brass box, Fig. 182, Plate XXVII, and the large quadrangular bell, Figs. 281 and 282, Plate XXXVII. The half-moons are inlaid or plated in copper on the brass. The edges of the object are ornamented with a band of plain guilloche pattern incised. It is possible that this might be a degenerate representation of a double-coiled mud-fish, as shown on the bronze ægis, Fig. 276, Plate XXXVI, and on the bronze necklet, Fig. 158, Plate XXV.

Fig. 227.—Necklet of agate and coral beads. Said to have belonged to the King of Benin.

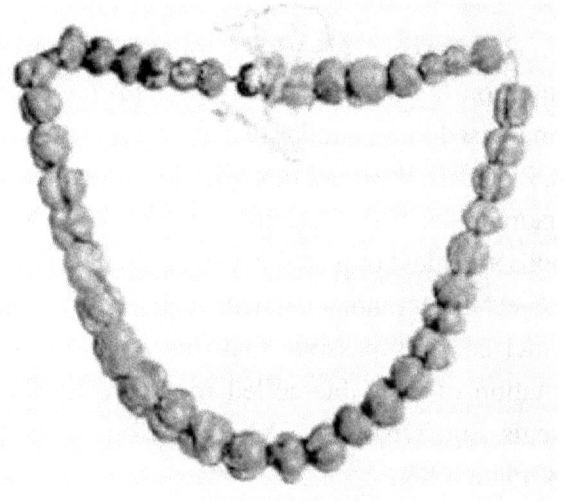

Fig. 228.—Armlet of coral beads.

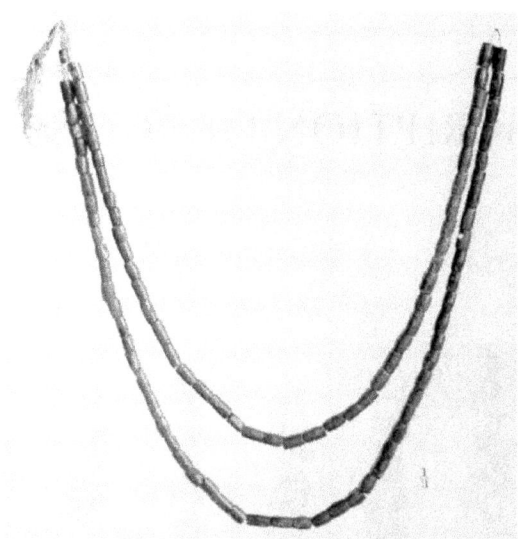

Fig. 229.—Necklace of agate cylindrical beads.

DESCRIPTION OF PLATE XXXI.

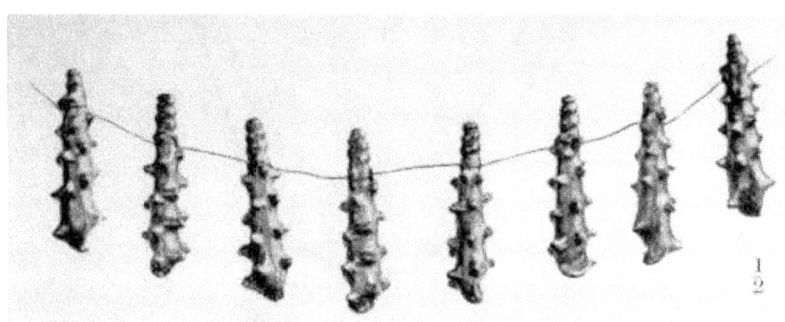

Fig. 230.—Eight shells of bronze gilt, forming part of a necklace.

Fig. 231.—Ten gold shells, which formed part of the King of Benin's necklace. The shells appear to be "cerithidæ." They are cast hollow. The weight of the ten is 8¾ ounces.

Figs. 232 to 234.—Bronze statuette, representing a figure standing; with broad leaf-shaped sword, similar to Figs. 326, 327, 328 and 329, having a twisted ring pommel in right hand, and a sistrum in left hand. Coral choker, badge of rank. Three tribal marks over each eye. Agate head-dress, similar to Fig. 121, Plate XXI, and curved agate pendants on each side. A large twisted ring rises out of the head-dress, which looks as if intended to enclose some thick band of cloth or other substance to suspend it. The crown of the head-dress terminates in a thick cylindrical spike with a flat top, like Fig. 111, Plate XIX, Fig. 155, Plate XXV, and Figs. 167 and 168, Plate XXVI. The sistrum is ornamented with a full-length human figure, holding a staff in right hand and the so-called key or axe in left hand. Beneath the bowl of the sistrum are three projecting cruciform bars, and the upper edge of the bowl is ornamented on each side with two heads very rudely cast. Dr. Felix Roth, in the "Halifax Naturalist," June, 1898, p. 33, speaks of these projecting prongs as being used for killing victims for sacrificial purposes, but the fact of their being sistri is shown in connection with Fig. 181, Plate XXVII. Sinuous serpents cover the shaft and bowl of the sistrum. The leaf-shaped sword is ornamented, front and back, with small imitations of itself. The figure has bands, probably of coral, crossing on the breast. The skirt is ornamented with conventionalized human heads with long hair and rows of guilloche pattern. Ankles have coral anklets. The skirt is bound up in the usual manner in a band behind the left shoulder. There is a band of small bells round the hips, and a human head and a bunch of bells on the left side. This figure was obtained from the Liverpool Museum, in the report of which it is elaborately described and figured with three others like it. "Bulletin of the Liverpool Museums," Vol. I, No. 2, p. 59. There is a figure like this in the British Museum. It is of considerable weight, being cast solid.

Figs. 235 and 236.—Bronze figure of a native, holding what appears to be a flint-lock gun, but the hammer of the lock is broken off. The stock is ornamented with a debased human head. The figure has a leopard's skin on front and back, tail and hind legs of which are shown behind; the tail terminates in a square bell. Sword in sheath on right side and a dagger under the arm on left side, with small bags on both sides. There is a row of eighteen cartridges in the waist-belt in front. The cartridges appear to be stuck upright into sockets in the belt. A curved horn powder-flask is on the belt on the left side. Pleated kilt below waist-belt. On the ground, touching the feet, is a decapitated head and nine large pellets, perhaps cannon balls. The pedestal ornamented with interlaced strap-work, alternating with oval figures, in character resembling the ornament on the stock of the gun. It stands on a framework of curved bars, now broken. The breeches are ornamented with vertical rows of circles. Although this figure holds a flint-lock gun, it is undoubtedly a native, as three tribal marks are shown above each eye. The face is also prognathic. The head-dress seems to be of a woven material.

DESCRIPTION OF PLATE XXXII.

Figs. 237 and 238.—Armlet of ivory, ornamented with representations of human heads, birds and animals, carved on the surface, and also of degenerate elephants' heads, the proboscis, in each case, terminating in a human hand holding a palm branch; horses' heads; tortoises; leopards, &c.; all of the most conventionalized forms. Bands of crotals are carved at each end of the armlet. The armlet consists of two halves connected by a thin brass plate and copper rivets on one side and on the other by copper fastenings. The plate is ornamented by a floral guilloche pattern, similar to that on the central band of Fig. 140, on the wands, Figs. 209 and 211, and elsewhere. This pattern is figured by Messrs. Read and Dalton in the "Journ. Anthrop. Inst.," Vol.

XXVII, Plate XXII. The carved figures represented on this ivory armlet are of much greater rudeness than those on the bronze objects generally. Much weathered and probably very old.

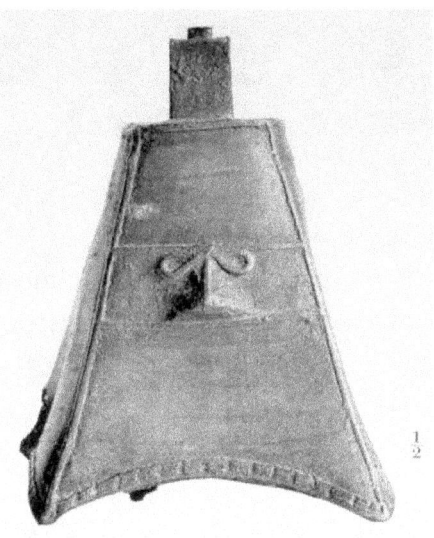

Fig. 239.—Quadrangular brass bell, with a degenerate face on one side; the eyes of the face are converted into loops.

Fig. 240.—Quadrangular brass bell. The loops on one side are evidently derived from the degenerate face on Fig. 239.

Fig. 241.—Brass bracelet, consisting of human heads linked together. One of the heads has projections ornamented with concentric circles.

Fig. 242.—Necklet of cylindrical coral beads, four of which are ornamented with straight line diaper pattern. One of the beads is ornamented with a guilloche pattern, with pellets inlaid with lead.

Fig. 243.—Brass bracelet, of peculiar form, ornamented with small circular punch-marks.

Fig. 244.—Brass bracelet, with clusters of rows of circular knobs or shells.

Fig. 245.—Brass bracelet, with six quadrangular knobs having red agate inlaid; similar to Fig. 38, Plate VII.

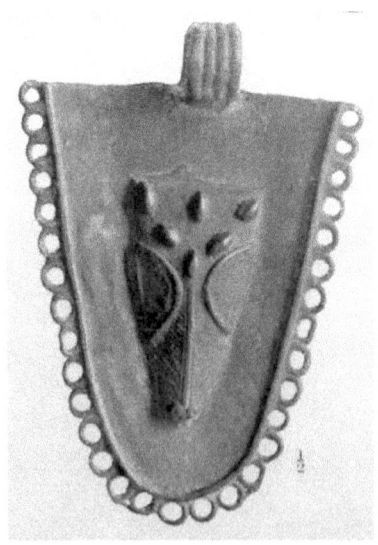

Fig. 246.—Ægis of bronze, representing a horse's head; edged with eyelets probably for suspending crotals, similar to Fig. 112, Plate XIX, and Figs. 126 and 127, Plate XXI. Engraved

on one side of the back is a broad leaf-shaped sword with ring pommel, similar to that on the Ægis, Fig. 276, Plate XXXVI. These engravings are peculiar, and seem to denote a badge or mark, perhaps of ownership of some kind.

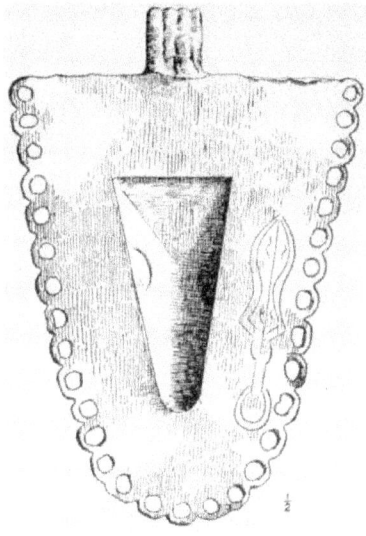

BACK VIEW.

Antique Works of Art from Benin 123

Fig. 247.—Bronze plaque, representing figure standing; weapon or implement resembling a ranseur of the sixteenth or seventeenth century in right hand, point upwards. Hair combed straight out. Pot helmet. Bodice fastened with three buttons and tags, perhaps armour. Left hand on left side. Band with clasp round waist. Pleated kilt like Fig. 129, Plate XXII; Figs. 235 and 236, Plate XXXI; Figs. 324 and 325, Plate XLII, and Figs. 360 and 361, Plate XLVI. This figure has very thick lips, but might not be negro. Ground ornamented with leaves in twos and threes, incised, and dotted punch-marks. The figure somewhat resembles in character the mounted figure, Fig. 129, Plate XXII.

Fig. 248.—Bronze plaque, representing a figure playing a drum with sticks; quadrangular bell on neck, ornamented with a sinuous snake, head downwards. Head-dress with two feathers. Hair combed straight and coiled in plaits. A peculiar kind of straight line diaper pattern on drum. This drum has pegs with nobs to fasten down the skin, similar to that represented on the

plaque, Fig. 181, Plate XXVII, and to the Jekri drum figured in "Journ. Anthrop. Inst.," Vol. I, New Series, Plate VIII, Fig. 5. Ground ornamented with incised leaf-shaped foil ornaments and punch-marks.

DESCRIPTION OF PLATE XXXIII.

Figs. 249 and 250.—Large bronze cover, use unknown; the ribs ornamented in the usual incised style of Benin work.

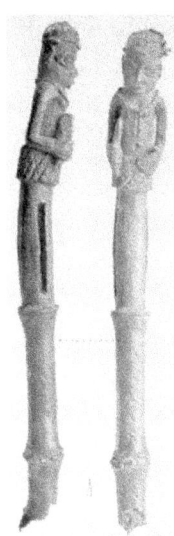

Figs. 251 and 252.—Top of a bronze mace, with slits resembling a crotal and a figure with an object, probably a neolithic celt, in the right hand. The figure appears to be bent forward.

Fig. 253.—Bronze round bell, similar to those attached to

the dresses on the plaques, Fig. 254, Plate XXXIII, and Fig. 264, Plate XXXIV.

Fig. 254.—Bronze plaque, representing a warrior, execution sword upheld in right hand; broad leaf-shaped sword in left, with a twisted ring or pommel. Quadrangular bell on neck, ornamented with a sinuous snake. Round bell on side; peculiar head-dress; armlets; object like a book under left arm; teeth necklace.

Fig. 255.—Bronze plaque, representing two figures, the right one having a broad leaf-shaped sword upheld in right hand, with a large ring extending from pommel; teeth necklace, but no coral choker; no bell on neck; cylindro-oval head-dress with feather on left side. Both figures hold the same spear, point downwards. Left figure with shield on left arm, quadrangular bell, and leopard's skin dress. Head-dress of the same form as the other, ornamented with cowrie shells. Skirts of both figures ornamented with human heads.

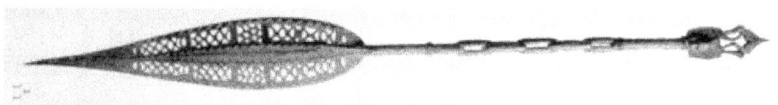

Fig. 256.—Carved wooden Jekri paddle, neighbourhood of Benin. Modern. Chain link shaft. Face on handle end. Pierced work blade.

Fig. 257.—Carved wooden Jekri paddle, neighbourhood of Benin. Modern. Chain link shaft. Full length human figure on handle end. Pierced work blade, with human figures, crocodiles, etc.

DESCRIPTION OF PLATE XXXIV.

Figs. 258 to 260.—Round execution block, with marks on the top for the thumbs and forehead of the victim; elaborately ornamented all over. On the projection on which the forehead is intended to rest is a double row of cowrie shells, bound round. A band of guilloche pattern, incised, runs round the circle, and the projections for the thumbs of the victim are ornamented with herring-bone pattern. On the sides of the block are three human figures in relief holding hands; shields, a leaf-shaped sword, and a trident points down. The shields are ornamented with straight line diaper pattern, and a band of the same runs round the top of the edge of the block. Two human arms and hands are on the side, and two boxes or stools are between the human figures.

The bottom of the sides is ornamented with a band of guilloche pattern in relief. The figures are clothed with jackets and skirts. The whole is much worn, as if by constant use.

Fig. 261.—Ivory horn, mouth-piece on convex side. Ornamented with bands of broken guilloche pattern.

Figs. 262 and 263.—Bronze plaque. A figure holding a so-called key in right hand. Coral choker, badge of rank. Head-dress, probably of agate or coral. No cross on dress.

Fig. 264.—Bronze plaque, representing a figure standing holding in both hands a leaf-shaped sword of the kind shown in No. 130. The sword is narrower, and the swell of the blade nearer the point than in the majority of specimens. A round bell is attached to the left side. The hair appears to be dishevelled and partly plaited. Three tribal marks over eyes.

DESCRIPTION OF PLATE XXXV.

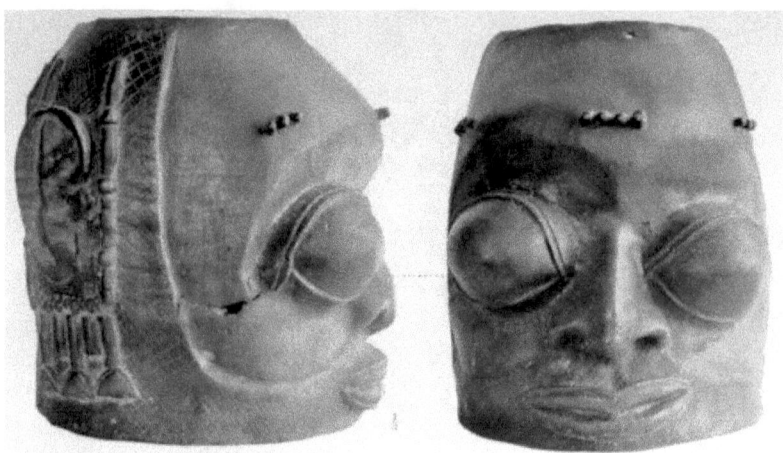

Figs. 265 and 266.—Bronze grotesque mask, intended probably as a stand for the carved ivory tusks in the Ju-Ju houses. The eyeballs project like those of the head, No. 137. Three tribal marks over each eye, and four over the nose. The forehead is very projecting; the nose aquiline and very broad. Tags, apparently of coral, are on the sides. The ears are very large.

Fig. 267.—Brass bottle and chain, rudely cast.

Figs. 268 to 270.—Long oval wooden bowl carved out of the solid. On one side (Fig. 269) is a row of five human figures in

Antique Works of Art from Benin 135

relief; the central figure has his hands upheld by attendants, who hold in their other hands shields having barbed javelins, points upward behind them. The shields are ornamented with straight line diaper pattern. Another figure holds an object under the arm, perhaps a drum or a food vessel. At both ends there is a representation of a degenerate elephant's head, the proboscis terminating in a human hand holding a branch, similar to Figs. 72, 167, and 316. At one end is a rude representation of a degenerate mud-fish. The other side of the bowl (Fig. 268) is ornamented with a broad guilloche pattern and a square interlaced figure. The interior of the bowl is very rudely chiselled out, showing marks of the tool all over. The carving is very rough and much in the style of the execution block, Figs. 259 and 260, Plate XXXIV.

Fig. 271.—Small bronze bird, with something in the mouth; very rude.

DESCRIPTION OF PLATE XXXVI.

Figs. 272 to 274.—Wooden comb, the handle carved as links of a chain, with a figure at top.

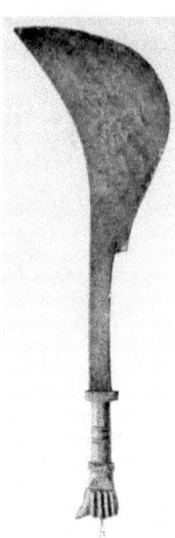

Fig. 275.—Small iron knife or bill-hook; the edge on the convex side; with brass handle terminating in a pommel representing a human hand.

Fig. 276.—Bronze ægis. Two interlaced mud-fish. This

perhaps shows the origin of the oval hole sometimes found on some of the objects, see Fig. 141, Plate XXIII, and Fig. 158, Plate XXV. This ægis has a broad leaf-shaped sword incised on the back of it, as shown in the annexed woodcut. These engravings are peculiar, and seem to denote a badge or mark, perhaps of ownership of some kind. The ægis is edged with eyelets, probably for suspending crotals, similar to Fig. 112, Plate XIX, and Figs. 126 and 127, Plate XXI.

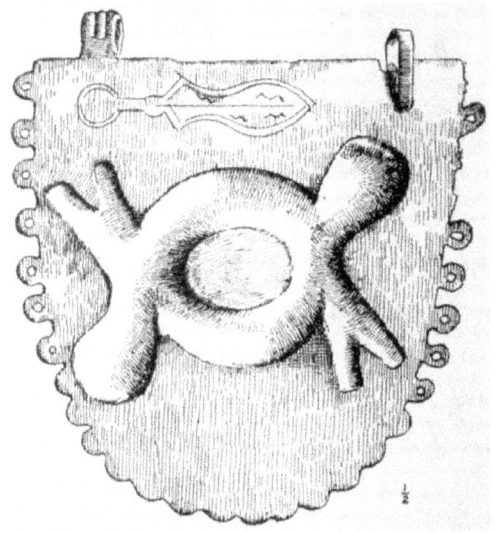

BACK VIEW.

Figs. 277 and 278.—Head carved in hard wood. The coral choker, the band round the head-dress, the feather on left side and the base are entirely covered with thin brass or bronze. Apparently intended to represent a cast metal head. Whether this is the case, or whether it is earlier than the introduction of metal casting, it is difficult to say. The face only and the top of the head-dress are left uncovered with metal. The top of the head-dress represents a reticulated head-dress of agate, like No. 121. The pupils of the eyes and the three tribal marks over each eye are of darker wood let in. There is a bronze band of metal along the forehead and nose. A ring of bronze-headed nails surrounds each eye. There is a broad hanging band on each side of the face, covered with thin metal and surmounted by a conical ornament. The metal is fastened on to the wood with oblong rivets. The face is extremely rudely carved. Round the base is a band of peculiar ornament in repoussé work, which is either intended for a floral ornament or a broken guilloche pattern, like that on the blades of the wands and elsewhere. There is a vertical hole through the back of the head, which is not large enough to contain a tusk.

Figs. 279 and 280.—Bronze rod, pointed below; perhaps the head of a staff intended to fit on to a wooden stem. Ornamented with a human figure sitting at top, with a human-headed staff in right hand, and a neolithic celt, edge up, in left hand. Coral choker and head-dress with serpents hanging head downwards, and a band of straight line diaper pattern. Three tribal marks over each eye. Band of guilloche pattern on skirt-rings for pendants (? crotals). Below, in a separate division, is a nude human figure kneeling and holding something in front in both hands. At sides sinuous serpents with the heads down, and crocodiles or lizards. Below again a sinuous serpent, head upwards. The whole very rudely cast.

DESCRIPTION OF PLATE XXXVII.

Figs. 281 and 282.—Bronze square bell, the ornamentation tastefully designed, with a human head, crocodiles, and floral ornaments. The clapper is in the form of a sinuous snake, head downwards.

Fig. 283.—Ivory armlet, very rudely carved in human figures, crocodiles, serpents, &c.

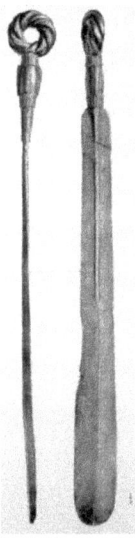

Figs. 284 and 285.—Brass or bronze sword, the pommel in the form of a twisted ring, as so frequently shown on the

Antique Works of Art from Benin 143

plaques, see Figs. 4, 113, 179, 255, etc. The blade is of unusual form, very broad, and rounded at the end.

Figs. 286 to 288.—Bronze plaque, representing a figure standing and holding in his left hand a staff with an eagle on the top. A staff with a bird on the top is represented in one of the figures of No. 139.

DESCRIPTION OF PLATE XXXVIII.

Fig. 289.—Bronze plaque, representing a human head with straight combed hair. Aquiline nose, moustache and beard; not of negro type. The ground ornamented with the usual leaf ornament.

Fig. 290.—Bronze plaque, with pendant fruit ribbed. Raised rosettes and the usual leaf ornament on field incised.

Fig. 291.—Bronze or brass plaque. Figure, full length; an unknown implement upheld in right hand, and an execution

sword held horizontally in left hand. Three tribal marks over each eye. The dress ornamented with human heads, half-moons, and floral ornaments incised. Ground ornamented with the usual leaf-shaped ornament.

Fig. 292.—Bronze ægis. A female with pointed head-dress, and coral choker, badge of rank; striking a sistrum with a rod. It is repaired with lead.

Figs. 293 and 294.—Bronze statuette, representing a negro figure holding a so-called key in the left hand. The figure has three tribal marks over each eye, and three radiating lines branching from the corners of the mouth. The pupils of the eyes are inlaid with iron. A cross on the breast hanging from the neck by a cord. No coral choker, but a necklace perhaps of coral or agate. A pot hat with a narrow straight brim. This figure exactly resembles No. 90. The ears are very rudely formed. No hair is shown. The face is very prognathous and the nose broad and flat, not aquiline. The skirt is only slightly hooked up.

DESCRIPTION OF PLATE XXXIX.

Fig. 295.—Bronze plaque, head of horse, very much elongated. For the elongation of a horse's head, see the figure of horse and rider in Figs. 299 and 300.

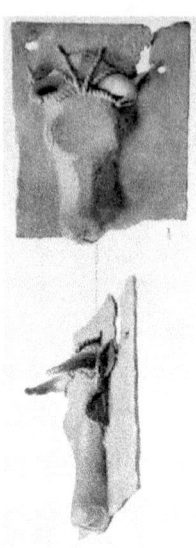

Figs. 296 and 297.—Bronze plaque, representing a cow's head, of natural form and proportions, with a rope bound round the horns.

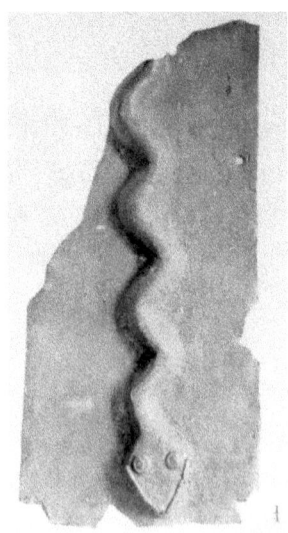

Fig. 298.—Bronze plaque. A sinuous serpent, head

downwards. Ground ornamented with the usual foil ornament incised.

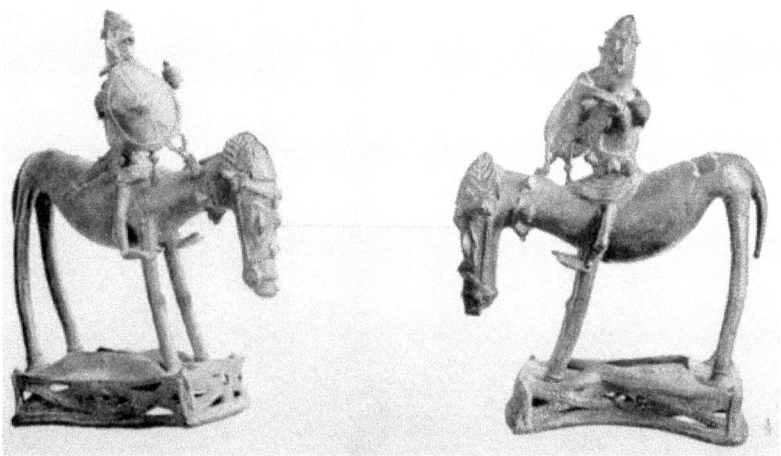

Figs. 299 and 300.—Bronze man on horseback, holding a shield, with barbed javelins, points downwards, on right arm. A band of crotals hung over right shoulder. Sword on right side with European scabbard. The dress is peculiar and formed with lappets on front and back. The horse and rider are very attenuated and rudely executed. The horse tucked up like a greyhound, with head very long, like Fig. 295. Band with crotals round the horse's neck. Large flaws in the casting of both horse and rider.

DESCRIPTION OF PLATE XL.

Fig. 301.—Bronze cock, the feathers represented by herring-bone pattern.

Figs. 302 and 303.—Elephant's tusk formed as a trumpet. The mouthpiece on the convex side; with rattle. The loose pieces of the rattle carved out of the solid, through the oblong apertures. Ornamented with three bands of guilloche pattern; straight line diaper pattern, and degenerate mud-fish interlaced, in two places.

Figs. 304 and 305.—Portion of an iron staff, ornamented with bands of bronze, on which are figured human faces, leopards' heads and bands of looped strands, similar to those on Figs. 139 and 140, Plate XXIII.

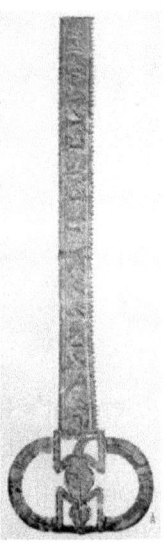

Fig. 306.—Thin brass head ornament for horse, and a broad band to go along the top of the head and mane. The figure on the lower part represents a crocodile, head downwards, ornamented with rows of copper rivets. The band for the head is ornamented with a floral ornament (floral guilloche) consisting of a sinuous stem with a leaf branching out of each curve, similar to that shown on Figs. 209, 238 and 278. The whole of the ornamentation is in repoussé work, and is probably intended to be attached to leather.

Figs. 307 and 308.—Lower portion of an iron staff, surrounded by bands of brass, ornamented with leopards' heads, frogs, looped strands and guilloche pattern.

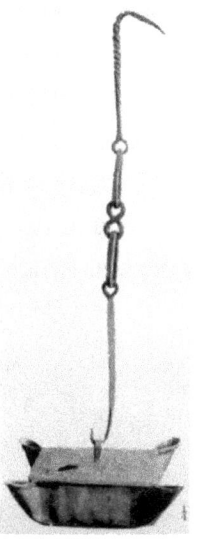

Fig. 309.—Square brass lamp, with four receptacles for

Antique Works of Art from Benin 155

wicks, one at each corner. Ornamented with dots of repoussé work, and suspended by an iron chain with long links and a hook.

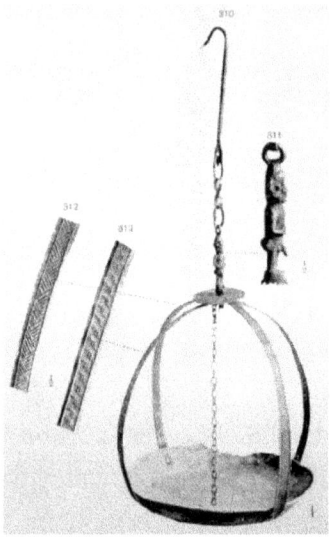

Figs. 310 to 313.—Bronze lamp, apparently with gold in its composition. The basin patched and riveted with copper. The bands for suspension ornamented with straight line diaper pattern (Fig. 312) and broken guilloche pattern (Fig. 313), united at top in a human figure (Fig. 311), having the private parts strongly pronounced. There are only one or two objects in this collection in which this peculiarity occurs, which is so prevalent in the art of most savages.

DESCRIPTION OF PLATE XLI.

Figs. 314 to 316.—Wooden stool, the top slightly basin-shaped; the stem carved to represent two interlaced serpents, but the interlacing is not continuous, being broken by a square hole pierced through the centre of the shaft. The heads of the serpents are conventional and they bend towards the top and bottom on alternate sides. The tails of the serpents terminate in the mouths of two frogs carved on the base and underside of the top of the seat. A human figure is in the mouth of the serpent resting on the base, holding a bill-hook in his left hand, similar to Figs. 108 and 109, Plate XVIII. On the underside of the seat, the serpent holds a leopard in its mouth; leopard holding a palm branch in its mouth. The other figures carved on the base and underside of the top are two degenerate mud-fish and two degenerate elephants' heads, the proboscis terminating in a human hand, like Figs. 72 and 167. The seat is ornamented with an interlaced guilloche pattern surrounding the top edge of the seat.

Fig. 317.—Wooden plaque, ornamented in the centre by a coil of interlaced strap-work, bounded by two lines of zigzag pattern. On one side a broad leaf-shaped sword with a ring pommel, similar to Figs. 326 and 327, Plate XLII, and Figs. 328 and 329, Plate XLIII. The handle is ornamented with a straight line diaper pattern. On the other side is represented an execution sword, similar to Fig. 110, Plate XVIII.

Figs. 318 and 319.—Wooden seat, of oblong form, supported by four legs, with cross-braces. All the ornamental portions are plated with thin brass, beaten on and riveted. The top of the seat is ornamented in the centre and ends by bands of single and double guilloche pattern, and in the centre of the squares by a square pattern of interlaced strands riveted on, similar to that represented on the blade of the sword, Fig. 199, Plate XXVIII. The legs and sides of the seat are ornamented by wheel-shaped forms, in eight places, and half-moons, similar to those on the ground-work of the plaque, Fig. 180, Plate XXVII. The stool in various parts is ornamented by brass-headed nails, which might perhaps be European.

DESCRIPTION OF PLATE XLII.

Figs. 320 and 321.—Wooden bird resembling a turkey. The inlaying of the eyes has disappeared; the feathers are conventionally represented by carved squares and lines of herring-bone pattern. On the top is a rudely-cut vertical projection 5 inches high and 2½ inches broad, the meaning of which is unknown; and from it hangs on each side of the bird, a broad band 3½ inches broad, carved with four rows of herring-bone pattern, the meaning of which is also unknown. The front of the base is ornamented with a guilloche pattern of four strands.

Fig. 322.—Circular brass fan, thickness of metal, .02 inch; ornamented with bands of guilloche pattern, herring-bone, and straight line diaper patterns. The handle is riveted to the fan.

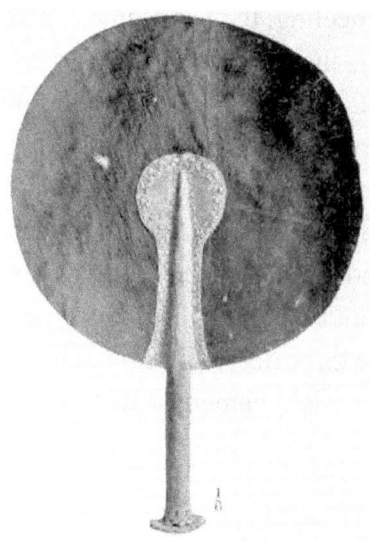

Antique Works of Art from Benin **161**

Fig. 323.—Fan of hide. The sewing of leather resembles that of the brass fan, Fig. 322, Plate XLII.

Figs. 324 and 325.—Bronze group of three human figures, the front figure kneeling, the hands in an attitude of prayer. The upper part naked, the lower part covered by a pleated kilt or skirt, similar to Figs. 129, 235, 236, and 247. The corners of the eyes ornamented with a raised barbed figure. A belt of two ropes round the waist with two loops behind, in one of which hang two links of a chain. This figure is attended behind by two short figures standing and armed with swords in sheaths. Coral necklaces and anklets. Three tribal marks incised over each eye. On the ground are three decapitated human heads, face upwards, and a dog. The base is ornamented with coiled figures.

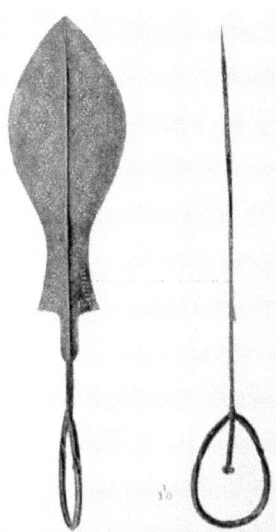

Figs. 326 and 327.—Broad leaf-shaped iron sword, similar to Figs. 328 and 329, Plate XLIII. The handle enclosed in a large ring of metal, 7 inches in diameter. The blade, which is .08 inch in thickness, is perforated by a pattern of holes.

DESCRIPTION OF PLATE XLIII.

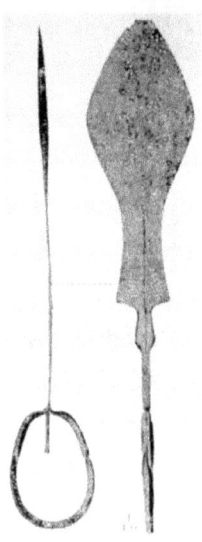

Figs. 328 and 329.—Broad leaf-shaped iron sword, similar to Figs. 326 and 327, Plate XLII. The handle enclosed in a large ring of metal, 8 inches by 5½ inches interior measurement, twisted in two places. It has probably had a grip of wood, which has disappeared. The blade, which is only ·06 inch in thickness, is ornamented with a pattern of perforated holes. The use of this instrument is unknown; it may have been an execution sword, but, if so, the ring-guard appears superfluous.

Fig. 330.—Iron staff, similar to the bronze one, Figs. 354 and 355, Plate XLV. In the cluster at the top is the figure of a bird surmounting an animal, probably a chameleon, similar to the one half-way down the stem, and surrounded by a cluster of various implements and weapons, points upwards, amongst which may be distinguished a fork with diamond-shaped heads, a curved bill-hook, a chisel, a spud and a reaping-hook. Below this are two clusters each of six hanging bells; two sinuous snakes, heads upwards, are crawling up the stem.

Figs. 331 and 332.—Carved wooden board, 10½ feet in length and 1 foot 11 inches broad; from a house in Benin city. It is ornamented with five panels in relief. Each panel has a circle with radiating lines, bounded by lines of guilloche pattern. The several panels are separated by broad bands of interlaced strap-work, deeply carved. The interlaced strap-work varies in design, some being simply plaited, and in others it is further complicated with twists and returns. Some have two interlaced bands, others four. The carving is irregular and traced by the eye without measure or T-square. Long sinuous snakes with heads are represented in the smaller lines dividing the panels and give the effect of a meander. The whole of the carving has originally been covered with thin plates of brass or bronze beaten on, traces of which are seen here and there fastened on with oblong rivets of metal.

Figs. 333 to 335.—Round execution block and stand of wood, elaborately carved with figures of men and animals. On the top is a pointed spike of wood, 5 inches in height, on which the head of the victim appears to have rested, and below this on the surface at the top of the block are two receptacles for the thumbs of the victim, in the form of coiled mud-fish. The ornamentation on the top consists of squares and triangles filled with parallel straight lines alternating in direction, and edged with a circle of broken guilloche pattern. On the sides are three human figures, two of which are holding hands upwards, weapons and shields, and one a curved sword of European form, point downwards. Between these figures are two boxes or stools; there are also two human hands and other objects on the other side. The bottom of the block is surrounded by a broad guilloche pattern of four or five strands. The stand on which the block stands is of semicircular form. The top is ornamented with two animals, resembling crocodiles, conforming to the outline of the curve, and other animals and objects. On the front of this stand is a row of objects, consisting, in the centre, of a human figure holding something on the abdomen, human hands, animals' heads, and other objects. A very similar execution block, but

Antique Works of Art from Benin **167**

without stand, is shown in Figs. 258 to 260, Plate XXXIV. The barbarous carving and ornamentation of such gruesome objects is quite characteristic of Benin art.

DESCRIPTION OF PLATE XLIV.

Fig. 336.—Wooden casket in the form of an ox's head, coated with thin brass riveted on. From the forehead two human hands rise up holding the horns. Along the forehead and along the sides are three lines of single guilloche pattern in repoussé work. The pupils of the eyes are inlaid with a dark substance. It appears to be a box or casket of some kind. A similar box is shown in the hands of the small figure in plaque No. 18, Plate IV. A precisely similar object from Benin is figured by Mr. Ling Roth in "The Studio," December, 1898, Fig. 18; and there is also another similar in the British Museum, figured in "Antiquities from Benin in the British Museum," Plate XI, Fig. 9.

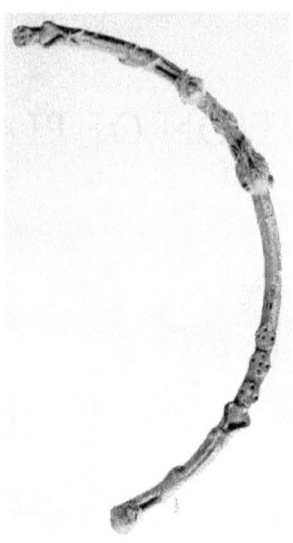

Fig. 337.—Half of a bronze circlet or necklet, similar to Fig. 158, Plate XXV; ornamented with two human forms with attenuated bodies and conventional heads, consisting of circles with five circular punch-marks to represent the features, and two other similar heads without bodies. The arms of these two figures are bound together at the wrists. At the feet of these two extended figures are two human heads of negro type, very well executed, and a leopard's head. It is ornamented in other places by a broad leaf-shaped sword and spirals. This remarkable work of savage art is shown in greater detail in the annexed woodcut.

Fig. 338.—Bronze sword, perhaps an execution sword, but rather too small for that purpose; with wooden grip and pommel. The blade is ornamented on both sides with incised semicircles and curved lines. The cutting edge is on the convex side.

Fig. 339.—Bronze sword, perhaps an execution sword, but rather too small for that purpose; ornamented with incised semicircles, like Fig. 338, and chevrons filled with parallel incised lines. The grip ornamented with parallel incised bands in imitation of binding. The blade is also ornamented with peculiar incised scrolls and circular punch-marks, and diamond forms.

Fig. 340.—Bronze pin, ornamented with four conventionalized birds. Inlaid in various places with red agate, and ornamented with circular punch-marks.

Fig. 341.—Bronze bell or sistrum, with small bell attached; both ornamented with an incised lozenge-shaped pattern. A similar double bell, from Yoruba, is figured by Mr. Ling Roth in "The Reliquary," 1898, p. 165.

Fig. 342.—Bronze figure of boy, with the palms of the hands erect and open, as if denying having stolen anything. Serpent, head downwards, on forehead. Three incised tribal marks over each eye. Coral necklace.

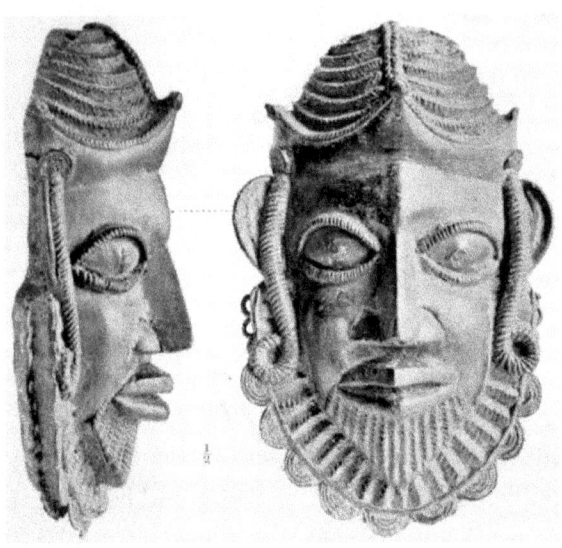

Figs. 343 and 344.—Human mask, of bronze. The pupils of the eyes inlaid with iron.

Fig. 345.—Bronze leopard, tail deficient; total height, 15¼ inches. One of the hind legs broken off and repaired by natives with a piece of ivory. The leopard is covered with incised spots and small punch-marks all over. The pupils of the eyes are inlaid with iron.

DESCRIPTION OF PLATE XLV.

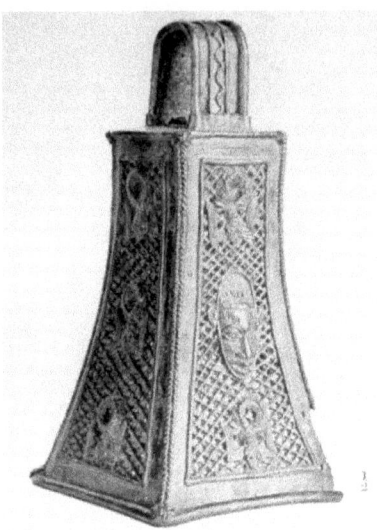

Fig. 346.—Quadrangular bronze bell, ornamented with mud-fish and a human head in relief. It is reticulated on all sides and could have emitted no sound.

Fig. 347.—Quadrangular bronze bell, ornamented on one side by a degenerate human face in relief. The ornamentation tastefully designed.

Fig. 348.—Bronze cock, somewhat similar to Fig. 301, Plate XL.

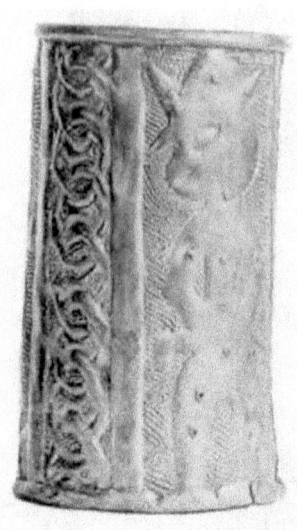

Fig. 349.—Brass armlet, made from one piece of thin metal, joined by copper rivets. Ornamented by three naked human figures in relief, and bands of interlaced rings.

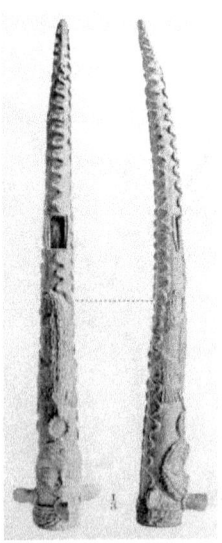

Figs. 350 and 351.—Bronze trumpet, slightly curved, the

mouth-hole on the convex side, similar in form to the ivory trumpets, Figs. 178, 192 and 193. Projecting blades, like celts, on the large end, as in the sistrum in Figs. 232 to 234, Plate XXXI. A somewhat similar instrument is figured by Mr. Ling Roth in the "Halifax Naturalist," June, 1898, p. 32. Above these blades is a human head in relief, surmounted by a circular ring held in the mouth of a crocodile, head downwards. Other parts are ornamented by sinuous snakes in relief. It appears to have been used both as trumpet and axe.

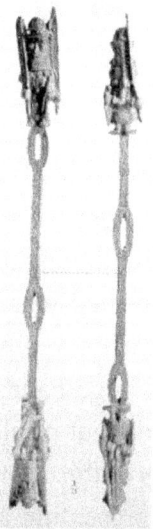

Figs. 352 and 353.—Bronze staff, probably intended to be held in the middle. Ornamented at both ends with human figures back to back. The stem ornamented with loops as in Figs. 208 and 209, Plate XXIX.

Figs. 354 and 355.—Bronze staff, 4 feet 10½ inches in length; ornamented at top with the figure of a bird with a small ball in its mouth, and apparently surmounting a leopard. Around it are ten leaf-shaped flanges ornamented with sinuous serpents, holding birds and crocodiles in their mouths. Below this is a human figure standing with very large hands, apparently clasped, and thumbs projecting upwards, out of all proportion to the size of the body; on the shoulders of this figure are two sinuous snakes. Below this are figures representing a monkey and a bull. The central figure is nude and kneeling with a cock in its hands, resting on a cluster of hanging bells. The lower part, which is broken and detached from the upper part, represents a human figure; in his left hand a large neolithic celt, and in his right hand a human-headed staff, similar in design to Figs. 279 and 280, Plate XXXVI. Below and in front of this figure are smaller figures, representing a human figure with a neolithic celt in the right hand and a spotted leopard, with tail curled over head, on the left. Rising from the head of the larger figure is an antelope, with two snakes springing out of its mouth, surrounded by representations of various weapons, points upwards. The whole appears to be constructed of bronze, surrounding an iron stem.

DESCRIPTION OF PLATE XLVI.

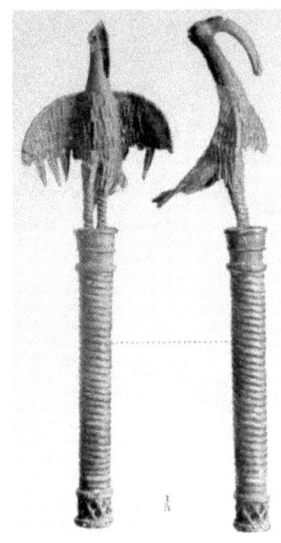

Figs. 356 and 357.—Bronze staff, surmounted by a vulture holding something in its beak, as in Figs. 286 to 288, Plate XXXVII; Fig. 271, Plate XXXV, and Figs. 354 and 355, Plate XLV. In Fig. 139, Plate XXIII, and in "Antiquities from Benin in the British Museum," Plate XXIX, Fig. 3, figures are shown holding these staves and striking them with rods.

Figs. 358 and 359.—Bronze seated figure, apparently of an European. The dress has large buttons on one side. The hat, with brim, is ornamented with chevrons filled with parallel straight lines; the moustache very long; the nose aquiline and very large; the shoulders guarded by "wings." Left hand and forearm broken.

Fig. 360.—Bronze or brass plaque, representing a figure standing to front, holding a piece of ring-money (Manilla) in right hand, similar to Plate XXI, Fig. 6, "Antiquities from Benin in the British Museum," where their use and form are discussed (p. 27). The dress has a single row of buttons, somewhat similar to Fig. 247, Plate XXXII, where however the coat is fastened with tags; the left hand is similarly spread upon the chest. The face is prognathous, but with hooked nose. The hat appears to be an European chimney-pot hat. Other cases of a pleated kilt occur in Figs. 129, 235, 236, 247, 324, 325, and 361.

Fig. 361.—Bronze plaque, representing a figure, seated, holding apparently a hand-cannon in both hands, the butt of which is curved down. The dress has buttons on one side, as in the previous figure, and is surmounted by a vandyke ornamented collar of European type. Belt and pleated kilt. Face, apparently European, aquiline nose. European helmet. European sword with guard on right side.

Fig. 362.—Iron axe, in carved wooden handle and shaft; with six wooden human faces, the pupils of the eyes inlaid with lead.

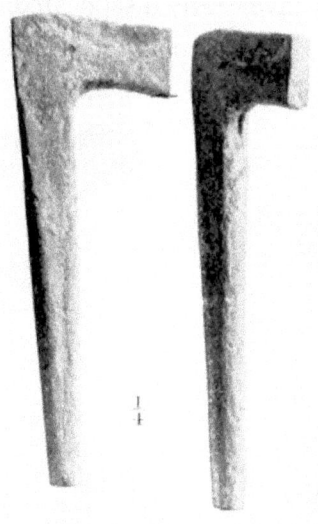

Figs. 363 and 364.—Iron hammer.

Figs. 365 and 366.—Small human head in earthenware, being the only one of that material in this collection. The pupils of the eyes are inlaid with iron; two iron bands on the forehead, of which the traces have nearly disappeared. Hole in top of head like those of bronze. Coral choker. The features are well formed.

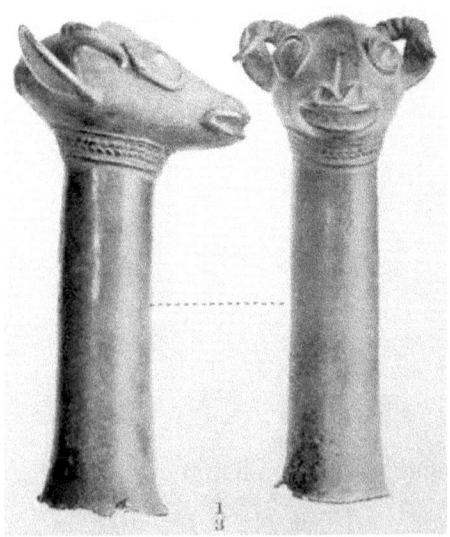

Figs. 367 and 368.—Antelope's head, in bronze, with horns and ears.

DESCRIPTION OF PLATE XLVII.

Figs. 369 to 371.—Bronze plaque, representing a sacrificial scene; it contains eight human figures, and a bullock just in the act of being slaughtered. All the figures except one have native features, dress, etc., and wear the insignia of executioners. The remaining figure is evidently intended to represent a European.

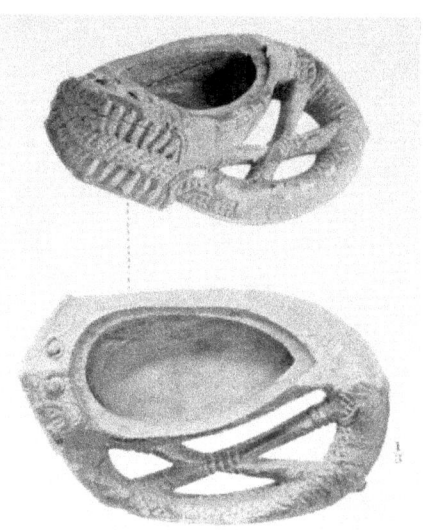

Figs. 372 and 373.—A carved ivory box in the form of a mud or cat fish. The eyes are inlaid with lead.

DESCRIPTION OF PLATE XLVIII.

Figs. 374 and 375.—Bronze statuette of a musician in the act of playing a wind instrument. He wears a pot hat, a collar, and loose necklet hanging down over the chest, also armlets and wristlets. He wears a decorated loin cloth, with a border representing a row of feathers, and in the centre of the garment is a conventional leopard's face. Height of statuette is 24½ inches.

Figs. 376 and 377.—Modern Benin sword; the blade is iron and decorated with incised birds and a nondescript animal. There are seven brass rivets hammered into the blade. The handle is covered with leather. Length of blade, 17¾ inches.

Antique Works of Art from Benin 191

Figs. 378 and 379.—Is a copper weapon which has had a wooden shaft. This weapon is of too soft a metal to be of much use.

Figs. 380 and 381.—An iron weapon of an old make. The blade is decorated with an incised figure of a snake. Length of blade, 21⅛ inches.

DESCRIPTION OF PLATE XLIX.

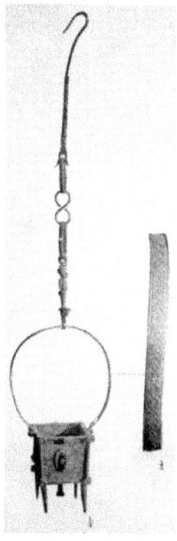

Figs. 382 and 383.—Cubical metal lamp, with handle, chain and hook for suspension. The hook is ornamented at its lower half with raised transverse incised lines and lozenge-shaped incisions. It is attached to a chain of three links, the upper and lower ones being oval; the middle one is 8-shaped. The other end of the chain is attached to a loop which projects from the head of a nude human figure (length of figure is 2½ inches), the feet of which are fixed by a loop of copper wire to the handle of the bar; the handle has a zigzag guilloche pattern on the upper side. There is a human face in relief on the sides of the body of the lamp, with fish-scale pattern on the groundwork. The borders of the lamp are raised rope pattern, and have a double loop knot

Antique Works of Art from Benin **193**

at each corner. The lamp has four legs, and from the centre of the bottom is a small round piece projecting, and not so long as the legs. It is capped with a circular bottom, which is decorated with incised concentric circles. Height from top of hook when suspended is 26 inches.

Fig. 384.—Metal armlet, ornamented with five rows of inlaid copper conventionalized cat-fishes and human faces; the latter have long hair, long whiskers, and long noses. Height, 5⅞ inches.

Fig. 385.—Metal box, cylindrical in form, ornamented with three longitudinal rows of ox skulls in relief, and incised human faces. Height, 7 inches.

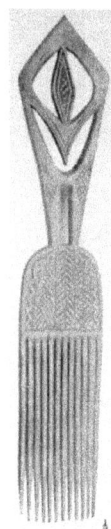

Fig. 386.—Wooden comb, with carved design.

Antique Works of Art from Benin 195

Fig. 387.—Cast metal bowl. The small opening at the top is situated in the centre of an incised rosette; this, together with four similar but smaller rosettes, are coated with a copper wash. On the base is a rosette within a circle.

Fig. 388.—Cast metal bowl. Distributed over the body of the bowl are eleven finely executed Maltese crosses.

Fig. 389.—Quadrangular bronze bell, ornamented on three sides with open reticulated work, framed in by a border of the guilloche pattern. A conventional face, with long hair and beard, is on one of the reticulated sides. Near the base of the ornamented side is a small roughly circular hole. Height, 6 inches.

DESCRIPTION OF PLATE L.

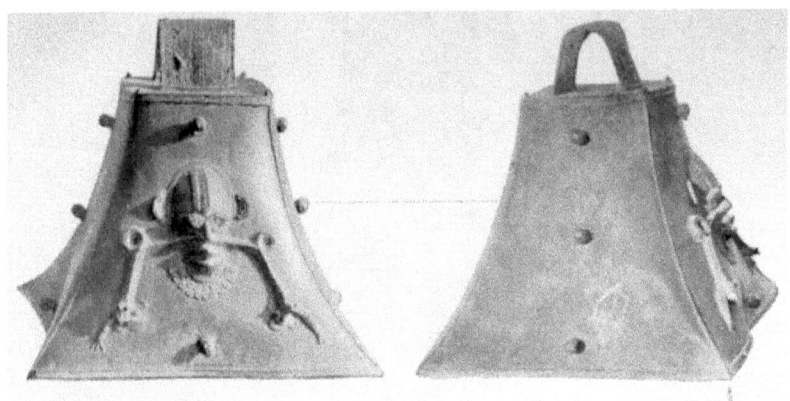

Figs. 390 and 391.—Large metal bell. On one side is a human face in relief, with snakes issuing from the nostrils. Each of the two snakes grasps a mud or cat fish in its jaws. The ears project from the sides of the head-dress, and the neck has a frill consisting of a double row of perforated circles. The handle has an incised herring-bone ornamentation. Projecting from the sides of the bell are eight knobs. The base and crown of the bell have a border of strap-work pattern. Height of bell, 10 inches.

Figs. 392 and 393.—Carved wooden head, which may have been a mask. Represents the head of a negro; it is hollow, and may have been intended for a mask, as there are open slits underneath each eye. The hair is represented by incised reticulated lines. The three black lines over the eyes represent cicatrices. The lower part of the face is rounded, and the chin not marked. Height, 13 inches.